Endorsements for *Building Culture the NASA Way*

"The success of any organization depends on the people. How do you attract, develop, and retain the best possible talent? That should be obvious to everyone, but the devil is always in the details. Brady Pyle does a superb job of providing those 'devilish' details with examples from his highly successful career as an HR manager—both with NASA and now with Space Center Houston. Every manager would benefit from Brady's lessons-learned!"

Michael L. Coats
Former NASA Astronaut and
Johnson Space Center Director

"Brady's deep experience and passion for effective leadership is evident in his latest book. He weaves together key principles, practical approaches, and illustrative stories to drive home the value of critical cultural tenets. Brady has witnessed and helped lead his organization through challenges so it emerged stronger with a more engaged workforce. This book is packed with helpful tips and useful suggestions to help any leader navigate and improve their team dynamic and larger work environment."

Scott Prochazka
Past President and CEO of CenterPoint Energy

"*Building Culture the NASA Way* needs to be on the reading list of leaders and HR professionals who want to make the right kind of impact with their organizations. Mixing insider stories of NASA with practical tools to advance the culture of an organization, I slowed down only to write down idea after idea that I was going to use myself. This will be a book I go back to again."

Jack Briggs
Major General
U.S. Air Force (Retired)
Former Non-Profit CEO

"*Building Culture the NASA Way* is a field manual for leaders who want to build teams that perform under pressure. This book gives readers more than inspiration. It also gives them a roadmap for action. Brady Pyle translates decades of NASA experience into a clear system any organization can use to align people, purpose, and execution. If you want to build a team that thinks clearly, moves fast, and performs with shared conviction, start here."

Dan Kasper
Former Navy Special Operations
Founder and CEO

"Brady Pyle has captured what every leader needs to know: culture drives success. In *Building Culture the NASA Way*, he offers proven steps to weave mission, vision, and values into the heart of every organization. This book will leave you energized and equipped to build a culture that inspires excellence and innovation."

Mark A. Griffin
Fortune 500 HR Executive,
Author and Founder, IHN HR

"*Building Culture the NASA Way* is a must read for any leader. Brady Pyle captures the unique experience and captivating stories of navigating through the space-focused environment and keeping the workforce not only engaged but also committed to the success of the organization.

"With lives on the line on a daily basis, NASA cannot afford to have teams that 'phone it in.' Ensuring the safety of everyone involved, at all levels, is engrained in the organizational culture. Through this book, Brady allows the reader to understand and learn from his experiences that are adaptable to any organization, as he has shown in his current role at Space Center Houston."

Denise S. Navarro
President and CEO
Logical Innovations, Inc.

"Brady Pyle's *Building Culture the NASA Way* takes you on a journey that illustrates how powerful a healthy culture can be when it's supported by dedicated leadership. Pyle does an incredible job of connecting the dots between purpose, performance, and most importantly, people, helping readers see that committed leadership isn't about titles; it's about trust.

"This book is an absolute must-read for anyone passionate about strengthening their leadership approach. It encourages leaders to take bold risks while safeguarding the culture that has brought them success. With practical strategies and a solid framework learned at NASA, Pyle offers a guiding template that can transform your culture from one small step into one giant leap forward, making a lasting impact on everyone you lead.

"Pyle also navigates timeless leadership principles with clarity and authenticity, reminding us that building a great culture isn't 'rocket science.' It's about commitment, genuine connection, and consistent effort when building a strong foundation in order to reach the stars."

Ricky Dickson
Retired CEO and President Blue Bell Creameries, LP
Author of *One Scoop at a Time*

"*Building Culture the NASA Way* is valuable to HR leaders at any stage of their career—from just beginning in the field to a seasoned HR professional. The book contains practical advice shaped from experience that includes trial-and-error examples. The result is a game plan that has been tested and implemented with examples of what has been effective along with the pitfalls one may encounter on the journey. It's a valuable resource for those managing the HR function."

Kenny Wagener
Global Management Consultant
Entertainment Industry

"Brady Pyle captures timeless lessons from NASA's culture that go far beyond HR. *Building Culture the NASA Way* offers practical insights any leader can apply to strengthen their team, elevate trust, and foster innovation. It's a concise, grounded guide to building organizations where people and performance thrive together."

James Bryant, Ph.D., P.E.
Executive Coach, Business Growth Consultant, and Podcast Host
President, Engineer Your Success, LLC

"Brady Pyle brings the clarity and discipline of a NASA leader to the complex world of organizational culture. *Building Culture the NASA Way* distills decades of experience into actionable insights every leader can apply to inspire trust, collaboration, and performance."

Trent Martin
New Space Aerospace Executive

"In *Building Culture the NASA Way*, Brady Pyle translates his powerful HR and leadership expertise into practical, human-centered wisdom. I've had the privilege of working alongside Brady through some challenging moments in our industry, and his servant leadership, strategic clarity, and ability to bring out the best in individuals and teams are truly inspirational.

"This book offers transferable, real-world lessons for leaders at every level—from aspiring supervisors to seasoned executives. Brady shows that even NASA's finest are always learning, always improving, and always building culture with intention. A must-read for anyone committed to leading with purpose."

Stephanie M. Baillio
HR Executive for an Engineering and Technology Company
Former Adjunct HR Instructor

"What a wonderful, informative, and easy read. The experiences and frameworks shared are informative and inspiring and should be leveraged by HR pros and leaders at all levels and career stages. This is superb work!"

Thomas J. Lopez
HR Leader, Entrepreneur, and Content Creator

"Brady Pyle delivers a rare combination of inspiration and practicality. *Building Culture the NASA Way* translates decades of NASA wisdom into clear, actionable lessons for leaders who want to align people, purpose, and performance."

Brian Friedman
Strategy Director of Benivo
Host of *The View from the Top* Livecast

"Brady has had a long and distinguished career as a human resources executive at NASA and now is a key leader outside of the government. Brady's experience and insights have proven invaluable to those of us who have had the pleasure of working with him. He has demonstrated over and over that he can bring a unique perspective, positive change, and value to any team or situation."

John Sims
Retired NASA Mission Operations and
Human Health and Performance Executive Leader

"The way Brady connects organizational culture to his NASA experience brings the topic of *Building Culture the NASA Way* to life in a practical way. His stories and insights help readers see that great culture doesn't happen by accident; it's built on purpose with discipline and shared values. This book gives leaders the tools and understanding they need to guide their teams toward health, stability, and mission-focused success. If you lead people, this book should be on your bookshelf."

Darin Griffiths
Vice President of Counseling Ministry
STCH Ministries Family Counseling

"Brady Pyle's *Building Culture the NASA Way* provides a clear and practical blueprint for achieving success within even the most complex organizations. I applaud Brady for equipping leaders with a valuable tool that helps them navigate culture, tackle challenges, and ultimately guide their teams toward meaningful results."

J. Kevin Hand
CEO of Hand & Associates, Inc.

"Brady Pyle takes you on a fascinating cultural journey inside one of the most intriguing organizations in history—NASA—and provides very practical tools to apply lessons and avoid pitfalls within your own teams. He knows it because he lived it, led it, and is now successfully building culture outside the agency."

Phil West
Corporate Communications Executive

"Through the imaginative lens of a NASA space mission, Brady shares his career story so others can benefit from his growth as an HR practitioner and his insights into shaping organizational culture. The narrative flows easily—making it a quick and engaging read—while the practical 'how to' lists and examples are packed with ideas and references. This playbook offers a seasoned perspective that's both aspirational and refreshingly down-to-earth."

Jane Datta
Former NASA Chief Human Capital Officer

"We can all learn from the NASA way and from Brady's experiences. The insights and lessons shared are practical and easily accessible—offering key takeaways for people leaders."

LaTanya Flix
Inclusive Leadership Executive, Culture Architect, and Certified Coach

"Brady and I worked together for many years and developed a strong partnership supporting a high-performing workforce. Brady does an excellent job describing his professional journey, demonstrating his continued commitment to growth and learning, and how his NASA tenure enabled him to reach for the stars! This book offers compelling reasons and practical strategies in addressing your organizational culture to increase performance outcomes."

Natalie Saiz
Former NASA Executive and Co-Founder, Stellar Leadership

Building Culture the NASA Way

Mission-Critical Principles for Creating Any Organization's Culture

Brady Pyle

Retired NASA Executive

Foreword by
Veteran Astronaut Dr. Ellen Ochoa

Copyright © 2026 by Brady Pyle
First Hardback and Paperback Edition

All rights reserved. No part of this publication may be reproduced, distributed, or transmitted in any form or by any means, including photocopying, recording, or other electronic or mechanical methods, without the prior written permission of the publisher, except in the case of brief quotations embodied in critical reviews and certain other noncommercial uses permitted by copyright law. For permission requests, write to the publisher, addressed "Attention: Permissions Coordinator," at the address below.

Some names, businesses, places, events, locales, incidents, and identifying details inside this book have been changed to protect the privacy of individuals.

Published by Freiling Agency, LLC.

P.O. Box 1264
Warrenton, VA 20188

www.FreilingAgency.com

HB ISBN: 978-1-969826-41-2
PB ISBN: 978-1-969826-40-5
E-book ISBN: 978-1-969826-42-9

Dedication

This book is dedicated to my small but mighty human resources (HR) team at Space Center Houston—a half dozen courageous HR professionals, who seek to Build Culture the NASA Way…

I couldn't have been prouder than I was in October 2025 when our team was named a "Top 50 HR Team" by the OnCon Icon Awards. These awards celebrate organizations making a measurable difference within their workplaces and communities. The selection process involved nomination, independent review, and public voting to recognize teams demonstrating exceptional leadership, innovation, and influence in their fields.

Our HR "Crew" (yes, we like to use NASA terms in the Official Visitor Center for the Johnson Space Center) at Space Center Houston joined other prestigious organizations across the country celebrated for fostering engagement, supporting people-driven cultures, and advancing workplace excellence.

Also, many thanks to the senior leaders and HR colleagues I encountered over the last thirty years who have demonstrated how to build culture …

And a big thanks to my wife of twenty-nine years, Jennifer, who has supported my professional career and writing journey. Together, we thank our kids: Katy (and her husband Evan), Cody, and Tanner—all of whom provide inspiration for building a strong home culture too!

May these words help you and your organization

Build Culture the NASA Way...

Contents

Foreword by Dr. Ellen Ochoa xvii
Veteran Astronaut and Former Director, Johnson Space Center

Preface: How this Book Can Help You xix

A Note of Gratitude xxv

Flight Readiness Review 1
N: Navigate the Culture 3
Understand your existing culture, values, and dynamics

Launch 21
A: Assess and Adapt 23
Measure the culture and focus on the critical elements that drive success.

On-Orbit 51
S: Strengthen Leadership and Systems 53
Engage leadership to model and drive cultural change.

Re-Entry 89
A: Activate Inclusion and Innovation 91
Build a culture that prioritizes inclusivity and innovation, while effectively communicating progress.

Landing 127
It Really Can Be Done Anywhere 129
Applying NASA's Lessons at Space Center Houston

Afterword by William T. Harris.............................149
President and Chief Executive Officer, Space Center Houston

Inspiration for HR Professionals..........................153

About the Author..171

Bibliography...175

Foreword

AT NASA, WE KNOW how to solve problems. We pull together a small "tiger team" of experts, brainstorm ideas, test solutions, and then execute. Every day, we train for challenges by bringing together a crew, Mission Control, and teams of engineers to simulate complex, real-life scenarios.

But building organizational culture is a very different kind of challenge, or at least it can seem that way. Most NASA leaders are engineers by training, and topics such as culture or employee engagement rarely appeared in our coursework. In truth, this isn't unique to NASA: in most organizations, leaders rise through the ranks because of their technical excellence, not necessarily because they know how to build and sustain a thriving culture.

Brady Pyle, a longtime NASA HR executive and expert, shows that building culture is not so different from engineering after all. It's an endeavor in designing human systems that can be broken into phases, each with objectives, tools, and measurable results. In this book, Brady organizes his insights using the phases of a space shuttle mission, a framework that appeals to space enthusiasts like me while making the strategies distinct and memorable for all readers. Through examples drawn from his distinguished career at Johnson Space Center (JSC) and now as chief HR and inclusion officer at Space Center Houston, he demonstrates that culture, like a spaceflight, succeeds only when driven by purpose, excellence, and teamwork.

When organizations say, "Our people are our greatest asset," they must back those words with intentional action to understand, value, and nurture that asset. I was privileged to work alongside Brady and other leaders he highlights in this book, and I share a deep personal connection to the employee engagement journey he describes and in which he was an instrumental part. From my first leadership role at JSC, I saw that the partnership with HR professionals was key to performance and mission success. Over time, my admiration for our HR team only grew. Like our engineers, they constantly challenged themselves to learn, to innovate, and to lead—always with the mission and our people at the heart of their work.

Serving with the team at Johnson Space Center was the privilege of my life. I hope that your own journey, guided by the insights in this book, proves just as inspiring and rewarding.

Ellen Ochoa
Veteran Astronaut
Former Director, NASA Johnson Space Center

Preface: How This Book Can Help You

WHY IS *BUILDING CULTURE the NASA Way* for you? Simply stated, building culture is an engineering challenge of human systems. And what organization is better at solving engineering challenges than NASA?

As Peter Drucker (an American management consultant, educator, and author, whose writings contributed to the philosophical and practical foundations of the modern business corporation) put it, "Culture eats strategy for breakfast!"

In this book, you will find actionable ways to translate theoretical concepts into tools that propel organization performance.

Are You an Organization Leader?

As an organization leader, you need to build the right culture. This book will provide you with a unique combination of strategies with practical approaches, tips, and techniques to build culture the way NASA did.

Prior to my early retirement from the federal government in 2023—following thirty years of service with NASA, culminating in my role as deputy chief human capital officer, NASA was named the Best Place to Work in the Federal Government for eleven straight years. At the time of writing, NASA has maintained its leading position for an additional two years, as documented by bestplacestowork.org.

In the chapters that follow, you will see how your role as a leader is critical to driving the culture that will generate better results for your team and your organization.

Are You an HR Professional?

My thirty-plus-year career has been as an HR advisor to rocket scientists, engineers, astronauts, and senior leaders for America's space program. I have walked in your shoes, starting as an internal management consultant, delivering and leading HR services, providing advice and consultation, and striving for strategic partnership.

In 2024, I was honored by *HRO Today* as their L&D (learning and development) Executive of the Year for Lifetime Achievement. In 2025, my team was named a Top 50 HR Team by OnConferences Icon Awards. The same organization nominated me as a Top Culture and Inclusion Professional for 2026.

I'm humbled by such recognition and want to share lessons with you. This playbook provides instruction on building a culture that has been used successfully for many years, and I can assure you that you will benefit from these approaches.

PREFACE: HOW THIS BOOK CAN HELP YOU

At the end of the book, I offer a special word of inspiration to HR professionals who are looking to build strategic partnerships with their customers.

How the Book Is Structured

I began my career at NASA in 1995, during the height of the Space Shuttle Program. We were flying seven to eight shuttle missions each year. This was the only way the United States could send astronauts to space at that time. We all had lots of practice for our individual roles, and *everyone* played a part.

Throughout my early years at NASA, I learned that building culture is like flying a space shuttle—it's a mission-driven effort that requires excellence, teamwork, and alignment among multiple stakeholders.

I framed the book around the phases of a space shuttle flight. In each section, I share how we are translating lessons from NASA (with its 18,000 employees) to Space Center Houston. Its 450-employee non-profit science and space exploration learning center serves as the official visitor center for NASA Johnson Space Center, hosting more than one million guests each year.

We start the journey with a **Flight Readiness Review**. For the Space Shuttle Program, these reviews—involving experts from multiple disciplines—critically examined all flight systems to determine when the shuttle was "go" for flight. The reviews identified issues for resolution, and NASA always "sweated the small stuff" to ensure a successful mission.

Similarly, you must **Navigate the Culture**. To do so, you need to fully understand the history of the organization and key events that shaped the culture to determine changes needed for the future.

The shuttle then moves to **Launch**. The shuttle lifts off using its main engines and solid rocket boosters, accelerating through the atmosphere. What an exciting day! For organizations, we need to **Assess and Adapt**, measuring the culture to effectively focus on the critical elements that drive success.

Once launched, the shuttle moves to **On-Orbit Operations**, conducting its mission, which could include deploying satellites, servicing the International Space Station, or conducting scientific experiments. Organizationally, this is the phase where we seek to **Strengthen Leadership and Systems**, engaging leadership to model and drive cultural change.

The next phase of the space shuttle flight is **Re-Entry**, where it slows and descends, enduring intense heat while being guided toward a landing site. In this phase, the shuttle faces the inherent dangers of returning through Earth's atmosphere.

Today, organizations face challenges with diversity—with ever-changing demographics and multiple generations in the workplace. Diversity naturally brings tension, so this is the phase in which you **Activate Inclusion and Innovation**. It is key to build a culture that prioritizes inclusivity to attain more creativity and innovation, while effectively communicating progress.

Finally, we must bring the spacecraft home, as the shuttle glides to a runway and touches down safely, completing its mission. Landing is another exciting day when the astronauts return home safely. Organizationally, **Landing** is recognizing that you are on target with the desired organization culture.

However, the landing phase was not the end for the space shuttle (until its final flight in 2011). Following a successful landing, each shuttle was fully refurbished for its next scheduled flight. This is a good reminder that culture work is never completed. It is a continuous work in progress.

As the final section will show, it really can be done anywhere…

May this book serve you well as you shoot for the stars!

A Note of Gratitude

DURING MY THIRTY-YEAR CAREER with NASA, I had the opportunity to observe rocket scientists, engineers, project managers, and executives who took on some of the world's biggest challenges.

Each day, I learned something new about the space program, which inspired me to shoot for the stars.

To the leaders I worked with, the HR professionals I worked alongside, and the mentors who poured into my career, I sincerely thank you.

To the nearly fifty people who reviewed an early manuscript and offered perspectives to improve the message and bring clarity for readers, thank you.

To the HR team who truly helped build NASA's culture—when many thought it was just fine—thank you for your courage, your example, and your perseverance.

To the crew at Space Center Houston, thank you for your willingness to experiment and try new things to enhance our culture.

To the readers who will learn new strategies, adopt new approaches, and try new techniques, thank you. I would love to hear what resonated with you and how your own stories of **Building Culture the NASA Way** unfolded...

Flight Readiness Review

A FLIGHT READINESS REVIEW (FRR) is a comprehensive meeting held before each space shuttle launch where all aspects of the mission, including the spacecraft, crew, ground systems, and launch procedures, are thoroughly reviewed to determine if the flight is ready to proceed safely and successfully. Essentially, it's a final check to ensure everything is in order before launch.

The purpose of the FRR is to identify any potential issues or concerns that could affect the flight and to make a "go" or "no-go" decision regarding launch based on the review findings.

A wide range of representatives provides perspectives from various teams including engineering, operations, safety, mission management, and the flight crew.

Each team presents status reports on its respective areas of responsibility, highlighting open items and concerns.

As the team converges on a particular decision, NASA takes special care to hear different viewpoints or dissenting opinions from the proposed decision.

At the end of the review, a consensus decision is reached regarding the readiness for launch, with a "go" signifying approval to proceed.

For organizations, we need to consider our own Flight Readiness Review. To do so, we need to start with an understanding of our organization's history and how the culture was shaped.

Just as a Flight Readiness Review invites and encourages different perspectives, we need to involve multiple perspectives, including technical representatives (at NASA, it was scientists and engineers), project management, financial professionals, business professionals, front-line leaders, and executives.

As Winston Churchill famously quipped, "Those who fail to learn from history are doomed to repeat it." Therefore, organizations must ask themselves, "What do we want repeated?" and "What do we *not* want to repeat?" The more we understand our organization's past, the better positioned we will be to guide it in a healthy direction.

This method played an essential role in shaping our team's culture at NASA.

N: Navigate the Culture

Understand your existing culture, values, and dynamics.

TO BUILD A SUCCESSFUL culture, you must navigate and deeply understand the existing culture. This involves recognizing values, beliefs, behaviors, and practices that have shaped the organization's history through both successes and failures.

On Saturday morning, February 1, 2003, I stared incredulously at the television. Reports were coming in that NASA lost communications with the space shuttle *Columbia*, and it was not landing in Florida as expected.

The day before—Friday, January 31, 2003—the NASA Johnson Space Center's (JSC's) engineering director and I met with the entire engineering leadership team in Houston to share a strategy of rightsizing the organization. For the first time in fifteen years, the organization's engineering staff would drop below 800, with plans to reduce to around 700 over five years as the focus shifted from supporting the space shuttle and International Space Station to multiple human space flight programs.

Still stunned while watching TV that Saturday morning, I turned to my wife—the mother of our two young children, ages three and almost one—and said, "I'm uncertain about NASA's future, and I'm not sure if I'll keep my job."

Why was the future so uncertain? Less than ten years earlier, the U.S. Congress engaged in significant debates about the future of NASA. In fact, the International Space Station (ISS) survived critical votes that threatened to end the program, narrowly securing its future. The ISS faced significant scrutiny and opposition due to concerns about escalating costs and doubts about its scientific value.

So, here we were, staring in the face of a significant accident that would impact the future of both the space shuttle and ISS. Later in the day on February 1, 2003,

President George W. Bush addressed the nation. He captured the sentiment at NASA well when he said, "We have lost seven astronauts—a husband, a wife, sons and daughters, friends. They knew the dangers of space travel, yet they also knew the importance of discovery."

President Bush went on to say, "The cause in which they died will continue. America's space program will go on."

The nation once again rallied in support of NASA—just as it had done following the previous space shuttle *Challenger* accident.

How Did I Get Here?

Since the ninth grade, I wanted to pursue a career in government service like my father and grandfather, who both were public servants with the Corpus Christi (Texas) Army Depot.

After serving a couple of cooperative education work tours for the Department of Health and Human Services (HHS) human resources (HR) offices in Dallas, Texas, and Washington, D.C., I knew that I wanted a career in HR.

As a graduate student, I conducted a study of the federal government's HR jobs in Texas and ultimately secured another cooperative education opportunity with NASA's Johnson Space Center. Since I was not very familiar with the space program at the time, I didn't fully grasp what a unique experience this was. As I approached graduation, hiring at the Johnson Space Center was very limited. I was fortunate to be one of ten students who received full-time permanent job offers in 1996.

I quickly learned NASA's culture, which is based on its core values:

- Safety: Ensure all systems are safe, reliable, and secure.
- Integrity: Adhere to high standards of integrity.
- Teamwork: Work together to achieve goals.
- Excellence: Strive for excellence in everything they do.

NASA's core values were congruent with my own, which were shaped by my grandfather and father:

- Integrity: Do what you say.
- Excellence: Do your best.
- Improvement: Get better over time.

It was a great person-job fit.

Why Is NASA in Texas?

"We choose to go to the moon in this decade and do the other things, not because they are easy, but because they are hard."
   President John F. Kennedy, September 12, 1962

When President John F. Kennedy set his sights on sending astronauts to the moon, NASA began searching for the perfect location to base its manned spaceflight activities. After a nationwide search, Houston, Texas, emerged as the preferred site. The choice was influenced by the city's access to universities for research collaboration, a strong local aerospace sector, favorable weather that enabled operations all year, and the significant political support from Texan Vice President Lyndon Baines Johnson.

Rice University donated 1,000 acres of land in Clear Lake, southeast of downtown Houston, which were well-suited for a large, state-of-the-art space center. The Manned Spacecraft Center was built to support astronaut training, spacecraft development, mission planning, and real-time mission control for crewed spaceflights. In 1973, following the death of President Lyndon Johnson, the center was renamed in his honor.

Since its founding, NASA Johnson Space Center has played a pivotal role in human space exploration, becoming synonymous with America's crewed spaceflight missions and earning a place in history for its contributions to such achievements as the Apollo moon landings and the space shuttle.

From its earliest days, JSC culture was marked by a bias for action and achieving what was previously considered impossible. In fact, "making the impossible possible" became a mantra for NASA.

International Space Station (ISS)

During my career, the cornerstone of human space exploration was the International Space Station.

From 1995 to 1998, downsizing and International Space Station assembly schedule slips had an adverse impact on workforce morale and stress levels. As the ISS human resources representative, I was challenged to provide the management team with advice and counsel on how to retain key talent. We engaged the management team in discussions of Beverly Katy's *Love 'Em or Lose 'Em: Getting Good People to Stay*, focusing on strategies to drive employee engagement and how to keep top talent from leaving. As a result of these discussions, the plans we pursued cut attrition in half—from 15 to 7 percent within a year.

By November 1998, morale was restored, and the team completed the first International Space Station assembly flight. Two years later, on November 2, 2000, the first crew to live on the International Space Station arrived, and a crew has lived aboard the ISS ever since.

The ISS proved the benefits of international collaboration with major technological contributions from Russia, Europe, Japan, and Canada. In fact, the ISS served as a symbol of post–Cold War cooperation and was an essential tool for fostering peaceful international relations.

To foster partnership, leaders recognized the importance of honoring different cultures and adjusting work styles to be more collaborative. NASA recognized the importance of honoring diversity and teamwork with others who did not share the same values, perspectives, and experiences.

N: NAVIGATE THE CULTURE

It is the diversity in backgrounds, culture, and technical competencies across various countries that significantly enhance ISS capabilities. To effectively engage with its partners, NASA intentionally sought to understand Russian culture and language needed to fly ISS. Additionally, NASA astronauts, engineers, and operators learned languages and cultures of the other key international partners as well. Learning how others approached spacecraft development and operations played a key role in NASA adapting its own strategies and approaches.

As a result of these efforts, the ISS became a landmark achievement in international space cooperation and a hub for scientific research and innovation. As the cornerstone of human space exploration, this international partnership of fifteen countries enabled crews of six to eight people to live continuously in space for more than twenty-five years in a spacecraft the length of a football field and the size of a five-bedroom house circling the earth at 17,500 miles per hour 200 miles above Earth.

As of early-2026, the orbiting laboratory continues to be a hub for scientific research and technology development. To date, more than 4,000 experiments have been conducted, involving researchers from more than 100 countries.

Government/Industry Relationships

In 2002, retired U.S. Marine Corps Lieutenant General Jefferson Davis "Beak" Howell became director of NASA Johnson Space Center—the first federal government contractor to fill this critical role.

As a contractor leader, Howell saw "a lot of flaws" and an opportunity for an integrated leadership team at the center. Shortly after he started, Howell focused on the relationship between the government and the contractor community, creating the JSC Joint Leadership Team.

This was an instrumental move in creating a single "JSC Team" mindset across the workforce, which comprised 3,000 government employees and 12,000 contractors. The JSC Joint Leadership Team was a critical new way of engaging leadership and provided a key foundation for what was soon to come.

Commercial Space

In the late 2000s, NASA initiated a new approach to commercial partnerships, initially through cargo transportation services to the ISS. Elon Musk's company SpaceX flourished in this program.

NASA then started to contract private companies to ferry astronauts to and from the ISS. This shift enabled NASA to buy crew transportation as a service, freeing it to focus on big-ticket exploration missions to the moon and Mars.

Now, NASA is pushing a new phase, encouraging commercial space stations to operate in low-earth orbit, eventually replacing the ISS. NASA's shifting role—from owner-operator to anchor customer—is stimulating a commercial economy in low-earth orbit.

The private industry brings scale, innovation, and investment to space exploration like never before, and this new approach required NASA to work with commercial entities in a new way to establish a commercial space ecosystem.

Critical Moments Shaping NASA Culture

In perhaps NASA's most iconic accomplishment, astronauts walked on the moon with Neil Armstrong famously declaring, "That's one small step for man, one giant leap for mankind."

Lunar missions collected 842 pounds of moon rocks, revolutionizing our understanding of the moon's composition and geologic history.

The moon program inspired a generation of scientists, engineers, and explorers, setting a precedent for ambitious exploration projects aimed at returning to the moon and going farther in space than we have ever been before.

Driven by President John F. Kennedy's mandate, NASA's culture embodied a sense of urgency and a unified national mission. NASA culture valued creative engineering and calculated risk, acknowledging the high stakes involved in space exploration.

The successful execution of complex tasks such as the moon landings and safe returns of astronauts demonstrated unprecedented engineering capabilities and team coordination—both within NASA and with external contractors and scientists who built a close-knit community united by shared objectives.

After setbacks such as the Apollo 1 tragedy, in which three astronauts lost their lives in a spacecraft fire during a ground test, NASA's culture evolved to prioritizing safety, testing extensively, and learning from errors.

Apollo missions, especially Apollo 13—a failed lunar landing that led to a remarkable safe return of the crew to Earth, memorialized in a movie starring Tom Hanks—stands as a testament to NASA's unique problem-solving and teamwork. This culture of adaptability and perseverance remains a model of crisis management.

NASA's missions to the moon were marked by an adventurous spirit that pushed human and technological boundaries, inspired by a vision of space as the next frontier for human achievement.

N: NAVIGATE THE CULTURE

Overall, NASA's achievements were driven by a culture of innovation, resilience, and the determination to achieve extraordinary results. Its legacy lives on in modern space exploration efforts.

Former astronaut Deke Slayton wrote in the Foreword of *Suddenly, Tomorrow Came... A History of the Johnson Space Center* by Henry Dethloff:

> The history of Johnson Space Center (JSC) is a detailed chronicle of the U.S. space program with emphasis on humans in space and on the ground. It realistically balances the role of the highly visible astronaut with the mammoth supporting team who provide the nuts, bolts, and gas to keep the train on the track. ... NASA and JSC became internationally recognized as symbols of excellence both inside and outside government. ...
>
> Almost every astronaut and cosmonaut who circled planet Earth has observed that from orbit there are no national borders visible on this beautiful globe. All those fortunate enough to view Earth from the Moon were impressed. ... These observations by humans in space have had a profound effect on humans on Earth and provide a strong unifying force for international space exploration. So as tomorrow comes, people of the Earth will inevitably step into the Universe and become true space

people—citizens of Mars, the Moon, Venus, and beyond.

This view of Earth by astronauts from space has become known as the "Overview Effect." From a leadership perspective, this has great implications. Leaders need to step back and zoom out from what's right in front of them to see their teams, their organizations, and the larger context. At the end of the day—at least if leaders can zoom out to a view from space—they will all recognize that our world does not have natural borders. That begs the question, "How do we work together for the betterment of planet earth?"

Space Shuttle *Columbia* Accident

Returning to 2003 following the space shuttle *Columbia* accident, an investigation board found significant cultural and organizational issues at NASA that contributed to the disaster.

The report emphasized that NASA had developed a culture in which engineers and managers normalized risks that had been observed on previous shuttle flights. For example, foam shedding during launch, which ultimately led to *Columbia*'s destruction, had been seen before and was considered acceptable rather than being addressed as a major safety issue.

The board found that safety standards had gradually eroded over the years, driven by budgetary pressures, tight schedules, and management's desire to maintain a high flight rate. Safety concerns were often downplayed or ignored.

The investigation highlighted communication breakdowns, where engineers' concerns were not adequately conveyed to or addressed by senior management. A hierarchical structure made it difficult for lower-level engineers to be heard. The culture discouraged open communication and questioning of decisions.

Managers often made decisions in echo chambers, where different perspectives or even dissenting opinions were not fully explored or valued.

The board criticized NASA management for making critical decisions based on incomplete data and for not seeking additional information. Specifically, managers decided against obtaining in-orbit imagery of the shuttle to inspect possible damage from the foam strike, which could have helped identify the danger.

If NASA managers understood the extent of the damage, they could have chosen to attempt a rescue mission—which would have carried its own significant risks.

Space Shuttle Return-to-Flight Task Force Report

The Return-to-Flight report underscored that resistance to cultural change remained a significant challenge. Despite increased safety awareness, there was concern that underlying behaviors and attitudes had not fundamentally shifted.

The report stressed the importance of empowering engineers and other technical experts to raise concerns without fear of reprisal or dismissal. A strong culture of safety and open dialogue was essential to prevent future accidents.

The report emphasized the need for clear leadership and accountability at all levels of the organization. It further recommended that NASA leaders foster an environment where safety is prioritized over meeting schedules and launch goals.

NASA Administrator Mike Griffin responded, "We're human and we make mistakes, but let's at least make new mistakes." He wanted leaders and teams at NASA to learn from history, including the mistakes of the past.

These external reviews underscored cultural transformation as essential for NASA to ensure the safety of its astronauts and the success of future missions. The emphasis was on creating an environment where safety concerns could be freely expressed and appropriately acted upon, with a strong focus on continuous improvement and accountability.

The Columbia Accident Investigation Board and subsequent Return-to-Flight Task Force both found that NASA needed to increase its technical oversight capabilities. For JSC Engineering, this meant a significant change from the January 2003 strategy of rightsizing. My role as the HR representative for the engineering organization at JSC was to hire more than 100 new engineers to support the space shuttle's return to flight. We were able to get that done within six months, and less than thirty months after the accident, the space shuttle successfully returned to flight.

Watching the next space shuttle launch and return was another highlight of my career. This time, I felt part of it—the work I did to hire and onboard 100 engineers played a key role in ensuring the success of the space shuttle and the continuation of the International Space Station assembly efforts.

State of the Johnson Space Center in 2005

Four months after the space shuttle returned to flight, a new center director assumed leadership of the Johnson Space Center—Michael L. Coats. I helped prepare an onboarding report for him, describing the JSC workforce's commitment to safety, technical excellence, loyalty, and strong work ethic.

The workforce had a reputation for being highly motivated, capable, committed, and confident. There is a lot of pride in NASA and its history of exciting, challenging, and meaningful work. JSC demonstrated a proven track record of flying humans in space. The workforce has a "can-do" attitude to ensure mission success, creating a reputation for resolving technical problems and challenges quickly.

In sharing the bottom line with Director Mike Coats, we noted, "The mission comes first, and JSC is dedicated to get the job done."

Over the years, JSC culture was strongly shaped by a belief that its purpose was to "make the impossible possible." The team was marked by actively striving and setting aside any doubts. This "it can be done" belief made leadership uniquely respectful of and dependent on people to unleash their creativity and demonstrate unparalleled excellence, both individually and in teams.

Simply stated, building culture is an engineering challenge of human systems. Organization culture is not a soft, abstract concept, but a systematic, designable structure—much like engineering spacecraft.

And what organization is better at solving engineering challenges and building spacecraft than NASA?

N: NAVIGATE THE CULTURE

Key NASA Principle: Navigate the Culture

To build a successful culture, you must navigate and deeply understand the existing culture. This involves recognizing values, beliefs, behaviors, and practices that shaped the organization's history through both successes and failures.

At NASA, we asked ourselves some important reflection questions. I encourage you to do the same.

Questions for Reflection:

- What do you know about your organization's history?
- What are some significant events that shaped your organization's culture?
- What are the core values that drive decision-making and behavior in your organization?
- How do employees at different levels perceive your organizational culture?
- What informal practices or traditions—"unwritten rules"—exist, and how do they shape your work environment?

As we reflected on these questions, our team moved into action. Consider the following action steps in your own journey.

Action Steps:

- Study the past successes and challenges of your organization to learn from both.
- Analyze how your culture has evolved and identify areas needing attention.
- Conduct surveys, interviews, and focus groups to assess current perceptions and cultural dynamics.
- Hold regular town hall meetings or open forums to discuss cultural strengths and areas for growth.
- Review onboarding and training materials to ensure they accurately reflect and reinforce desired cultural attributes.
- Encourage cross-functional collaboration projects to break down silos and foster shared understanding.
- Recognize and reward behaviors that exemplify the organization's core values.
- Benchmark your culture against industry standards or best practices to identify opportunities for improvement.
- Develop clear communication channels for employees to share ideas, concerns, and feedback about culture.

Launch

THE SPACE SHUTTLE LAUNCHED vertically like a rocket, using solid rocket boosters and liquid hydrogen and oxygen engines.

The launch sequence went something like this:

- The space shuttle's main engines started six seconds before launch and had to reach full thrust when the shuttle's solid rockets—two large boosters that provided extra thrust to lift the shuttle out of Earth's atmosphere—ignited.
- The solid rocket boosters separated and parachuted back to Earth for reuse.
- The shuttle's main engines continued to burn until the shuttle reached orbit.
- The shuttle's external fuel tank containing liquid hydrogen and oxygen that fed the shuttle's main engine was jettisoned.

As with a shuttle launch, a sequenced and intentional approach is necessary for building a culture that will drive the results you want in your organization.

A: Assess and Adapt

Measure the culture and focus on the critical elements that drive success.

TO CREATE CHANGE, YOU must assess the culture, measure its effectiveness, and then develop the right strategies. Measuring culture can identify what aspects of the organization need attention—and how the environment is either supporting or hindering your strategy.

As you "Launch" your journey to Build Culture the NASA Way, you need to measure your culture…

Yeah, but You're NASA!

Now, let's be honest. How many of you are thinking, "Yeah, but you're NASA! Of course, you're the best place to work in the federal government."

Well, let me share something with you. The Partnership for Public Service began its Best Places to Work in the Federal Government rankings in 2003—the year of the space shuttle *Columbia* accident, and these were NASA's results from 2003 through 2011:

- 2003: 71.6 percent engagement, placing third in the federal government
- 2005: 69.9 percent engagement, placing sixth in the federal government
- 2007: 69.7 percent engagement, placing fourth in the federal government
- 2009: 71.7 percent engagement, placing third in the federal government
- 2010: 74.2 percent engagement, placing fifth in the federal government
- 2011: 72.5 percent engagement, placing fifth in the federal government

A: ASSESS AND ADAPT

Benchmark Best Practices of Others

When Mike Coats was named the tenth director of NASA Johnson Space Center in 2005, he came home. Coats was a former astronaut who flew on three space shuttle missions.

After his last shuttle flight, Coats retired from the U.S. Navy and NASA, and then he joined the private sector as an executive. When he returned to JSC, he told his leadership team that the center needed to change its "not-invented-here" reputation. For a long time, JSC was seen as an arrogant organization—employees often said, "After all, we did win the race to the moon!"

At every opportunity, Coats would explain to leaders that "success can be dangerous since it breeds complacency, and complacency can be fatal in the space business."

To accomplish a change, Coats required each of his direct report executives to benchmark with at least two external companies and share lessons they could use at JSC. Coats encouraged a new open-mindedness to strengthen the team.

Coats even spearheaded benchmarking initiatives to improve organizational culture at JSC. He led teams of senior executives to engage with companies such as Lockheed-Martin and Georgia Power regarding their approaches to diversity and inclusion. Both organizations provided insights on using employee resource groups to enhance talent attraction, retention, and engagement. Furthermore, they described distinctive leadership development programs designed to strengthen inclusive leadership capabilities. These findings were valuable for JSC's leadership and contributed to my own learning and growth as an HR professional.

A Different Approach

In 2008, as part of NASA's Leadership Development Program, I embraced the mindset of learning from other organizations. I seized an opportunity to work outside of NASA and gain a different perspective. For six months, I worked in the International Finance Corporation's (IFC) HR Department.

The IFC—a member of the World Bank Group, a public sector institution—had 3,200 staff members, and more than 90 percent of them had work experience in the private sector. Interestingly, the IFC strives to embody the best practices of the private sector within the parameters of a public sector organization.

During my time there, I conducted analyses of the IFC staff survey that led to follow-up action plans for all thirty-eight departments. What I found is that the level of detailed analyses and accountability required by IFC were unmatched at NASA. In fact, every IFC department had action plans for improvement, and specific attention was paid to the organizations in the bottom quartile.

Leadership at the executive level took responsibility for overseeing IFC-wide follow-up actions. Observing another organization's deliberate efforts to shape its culture was particularly noteworthy to my own professional growth and development.

A Change in NASA Leadership

When Charles Bolden, Jr.—a former astronaut who flew on four space shuttle missions and retired as a major general from the United States Marine Corps—was named NASA's twelfth administrator in 2009, he did not believe NASA's rankings among the Best Places to Work in the Federal Government were acceptable.

As a Marine Corps leader, Bolden's approach was to both accomplish the mission and take care of the people. He recognized that by improving workforce morale and engagement, he would enhance performance and mission success at NASA.

To partner with him on this strategy, Bolden selected Jeri Buchholz as NASA's chief human capital officer. Buchholz came to NASA from the U.S. Nuclear Regulatory Commission (NRC), where she played a significant role in shaping culture. In fact, NRC was the Best Place to Work in the Federal Government in 2009. NRC consistently ranked highly on this list due to effective leadership, employee engagement, and a strong organizational culture.

Buchholz's work at the NRC contributed to its reputation as a top-notch workplace, and she brought that experience and focus on employee satisfaction and organizational effectiveness to NASA.

Learning from the Nuclear Regulatory Commission (NRC)

NRC leadership leveraged annual employee engagement survey results to its advantage. First, they critically examined the results and identified three to five areas for organization improvement. Second, each regional leadership team used the data plus results from individual 360-degree leadership surveys to determine team improvements. Because the results were listened to, reviewed, and acted upon, an astonishing 89 percent of NRC staff responded to the 2009 survey.

One key to their success was that NRC leadership ensured clarity and consistency—in fact, all employees could articulate the NRC mission. Mission messages were delivered from the top through front-line supervisors.

NRC's leadership ensured that people felt valued. They encouraged diversity of thought and ideas, embracing inclusion and a collaborative work environment. Additionally, leadership recognized the key role of intangibles, especially work-life balance, as they embraced a new flexible working schedule to accommodate different needs of employees.

Leaders each had a reasonable span of control (generally eight to ten direct reports), so they knew people by name and created strong manager-employee bonds.

Employee and leadership development was a priority with a focus on individual development plans. As proof of this commitment, 70 percent of staff members were required to take at least 24 hours of training each year. New employees were assigned a coach and a mentor during their two-year probationary period.

Together, these efforts produced a culture and environment that propelled the Nuclear Regulatory Commission to be named Best Place to Work in the Federal Government in 2009.

Measuring Culture

It is critical for leaders and organizations to develop and review measures of culture.

The Gallup organization has been measuring organization culture for more than twenty-five years, interviewing more than one million employees and asking hundreds of questions about countless aspects of the workplace. Using the data, Gallup researchers searched for the items that the most engaged employees—those who were loyal and productive—answered positively, and everyone else—the average and disengaged employees—answered neutrally or negatively.

From their research, Gallup discovered how these twelve questions (branded the Gallup Q12) differentiated the most engaged workplaces from the rest:

1. I know what is expected of me at work.
2. I have the materials and equipment I need to do my work right.
3. At work, I have the opportunity to do what I do best every day.
4. In the last seven days, I have received recognition or praise for doing good work.
5. My supervisor, or someone at work, seems to care about me as a person.
6. There is someone at work who encourages my development.
7. At work, my opinion seems to count.
8. The mission or purpose of my company makes me feel like my job is important.
9. My associates or fellow employees are committed to doing quality work.
10. I have a best friend at work.
11. In the last six months, someone at work has talked to me about my progress.
12. This last year, I have had opportunities at work to learn and grow.

While Gallup's twelve items do not capture everything about the workplace, they do capture the core elements needed to attract, focus, and retain the most talented employees.

Applying Gallup's Q12

As an example of how widely applicable these concepts are, several years ago, my church wanted to take a comprehensive look at its staff morale and engagement to determine where improvements were needed. Since I used the Gallup Q12 tool effectively in interviews with employees at NASA, I conducted interviews of my church's staff members using the same tool.

From the interviews, themes and areas of focus quickly emerged, and we developed an organization improvement plan.

Over the years, I have found the tool to be extremely effective in quickly identifying the critical issues an organization needs to address.

Employee Engagement Survey

There are a lot of different ways to effectively measure culture and engagement. Another perk of my thirty-year career in the federal government was being immersed in the annual employee engagement survey for federal employees, comprising 100 questions. That survey measured employees' perceptions of whether, and to what extent, conditions characterizing successful organizations are present in their agencies.

Measuring the Culture at Space Center Houston

When I came to Space Center Houston in 2023, I was excited to bring my NASA experience to bear in this new context. Rather than supporting an 18,000-employee workforce, I serve as chief HR and inclusion officer (or CHRIO, pronounced "cheerio") for a smaller team, without the constraints inherent in federal government human resources work.

I quickly learned that Space Center Houston had not conducted an employee engagement survey since 2019—prior to the global pandemic.

Based on my experiences with both the Gallup Q12 and the federal government's employee engagement survey, we crafted a thirty-question survey focusing on the following groupings and themes:

- You and Space Center Houston
- You and your supervisor
- You and our crew (employees at Space Center Houston)
- Belonging and accessibility
- Overall satisfaction

Then we asked this open-ended question: "What would make Space Center Houston an even better place to work?" As you might expect, this brief, simple survey provided rich quantitative and qualitative data to explore.

Focus on the Critical Few

Once the survey results are available, you need to analyze the data for themes. You may even need to convene focus groups of employees to determine the "critical few" areas of focus.

A Front-Line Leader in Engineering?

Permit me to reminisce a bit. After serving as deputy HR director at JSC for three years, I read *The Chief HR Officer* by Patrick Wright and learned that 70 percent of private sector HR leaders spent time outside HR functions.

Since my entire career had been in HR, I recognized the need for different experiences to be better prepared for future HR leadership roles. At the same time, NASA was discussing the criticality of the front-line leader's role in both organizational culture and employee engagement. I sought to gain a front-line leader's perspective as a branch-level leader for JSC's engineering organization. My challenge was to use my technical credibility in HR and leadership to address significant morale and employee engagement challenges.

Since measurable results were key, I used Gallup's Q12 questions to conduct one-on-one interviews with each of the team's twenty-four employees and quickly assessed what was going well and what needed to improve. These interviews revealed several leadership and management issues, including:

- Half of the engineering staff did not trust management.
- Management also showed little trust in engineers.
- Team lead roles and responsibilities were unclear.
- Employees wanted more direct meetings with management, especially for career advice.

I evaluated potential solutions and partnered with management to develop an organization improvement plan that clarified management roles and responsibilities and revised expectations for employees to show more trust in management.

I also worked closely with the supervisor and team leaders to clarify roles, responsibilities, authorities, and accountabilities for the team lead roles. The discussions were rich, as they came to more clearly understand their roles and expectations. As another key solution for the organization, I encouraged individual development plan conversations between management and employees.

Lastly, I facilitated a workshop based on the business best-seller *The 5 Languages of Appreciation in the Workplace* by Gary Chapman, which is designed to build a culture of appreciation across the team. I gathered everyone's self-assessment results and shared each team member's preferred language of appreciation, helping the team learn how to express gratitude more effectively. This boosted engagement within the team and allowed members to significantly improve work quality.

A: ASSESS AND ADAPT

The team responded well to the workshop, and my overall organization improvement efforts were recognized with a NASA award from management. The results were remarkable, as evidenced from the following employee engagement survey. Their Supervisory Index soared from 56 percent positive to 73 percent positive in just one year. In fact, NASA identified this organization as one of the ten most improved during that time. Ultimately, that organization became a case study for management improvements at NASA.

I have seen it time and again over the course of my career that focusing on the critical few and making progress toward improving the organization pays big dividends in engaging the workforce.

Determining Areas of Emphasis at Space Center Houston

Over my thirty years in the workforce—including twenty years of leadership and ten years in executive ranks—I have learned, observed, practiced ... and learned again ... a lot about leadership. One of those key lessons underscores the importance of a leader's first ninety days.

Listening Tour

Immediately upon joining Space Center Houston, I embarked on a listening tour, following the advice from Michael Watkins' book *The First 90 Days: Critical Success Strategies for New Leaders at All Levels*.

Watkins points out that leaders should set the tone by putting first things first, asking key questions from the best sources of insight. Make key decisions and deliver messages to clarify expectations. Create alliances and influence networks. Come out of the gate strong to build a team. Match the strategy with the situation.

Organizations are living, breathing systems, so you need to observe them from a variety of different perspectives and listen to their people to understand the current state before building plans and moving out on initiatives.

Human Resources (HR) Priorities

As a result of engaging with each manager and several employees at Space Center Houston, I gained a better understanding of the work environment and began to shape priorities for our HR team.

The major themes emerging from an employee survey and ensuing debriefs were clear—staff felt that pay was too low, and we did not have good salary transparency. At the same time, we conducted an external review of executive compensation. Our consultant pointed out that we needed to establish a clear compensation philosophy.

Based on the organization's growth strategy and position in the market relative to other non-profit benchmarks, we determined that we should pay in the top quartile. Our CEO and board of directors swiftly supported market-based pay adjustments across the organization that could get us to that target within three years.

Given the increased competition for talent, local market conditions, and our organization's outstanding financial position, I was pleased to let the team know that we could provide market-based pay adjustments immediately.

To improve transparency about pay at Space Center Houston, we initiated a project to develop a market-based grade and pay structure.

Talent Strategy

When I joined the organization, Space Center Houston was growing at a pace of about 10 percent per year. A variety of new positions and new capabilities was needed in the organization, so each new position was advertised externally. However, only 5 percent of new roles were filled internally.

My NASA experience was completely the opposite. Nearly 95 percent of promotions went to internal talent, and NASA used HR strategies that grew and developed employees, providing pipelines of talent to fill key roles.

I brought a new perspective to the Space Center Houston executive team and made the case for a talent strategy principle that half of our new positions would be filled by internal talent. I was pleased to see the enthusiastic support from the executive team, which led us to several HR priorities:

- Build a Career Development Guide with information on how employees can navigate their careers at Space Center Houston—showcasing career paths available across the organization and what it takes to move to specialist, manager, director, and executive-level roles.
- Provide regular, ongoing training opportunities.
- Improve visibility into internal promotion opportunities.

The Power Trio: HR's Game-Changing Responsibilities

I believe human resources leaders—and particularly my role as a C-suite HR executive—have three primary responsibilities:

1. Ensure workforce capabilities for the future.
2. Steward the culture of the organization.
3. Take care of the people.

Ensure Workforce Capabilities for the Future

A significant role of human resources is to ensure workforce capabilities to accomplish the mission both now and in the future. To do this, you need effective workforce planning. Incidentally, my first assignment as an HR executive at NASA was facilitating NASA's "Journey to

A: ASSESS AND ADAPT

Mars" workforce strategy, focused on the long-term skill and talent needs for future human missions to Mars.

Your workforce plan provides the context for talent acquisition strategies. Will you build, borrow, or buy talent to accomplish your mission? The workforce plan also informs strategies for talent development and talent management.

Steward the Culture

HR plays a key role in stewarding culture for an organization. The HR Handbook is filled with a variety of policies that influence culture.

Additionally, HR plays a key role in facilitating development of vision, mission, and values for the organization. Talent systems—assessment for hiring, training and development strategies, and performance management—all need to align with the vision, mission, and values to bring accountability for the expected behaviors that shape culture.

Take Care of People

Finally, HR needs to take care of the people through pay and benefits, recognition programs, and services that enhance employee health and wellness.

During my graduate studies in human resources management, I was introduced to the service profit chain framework. This approach suggests that when employees are engaged, they enhance customer satisfaction, eventually leading to lasting financial success.

Patrick M. Wright—the faculty leader responsible for our HR graduate program at Texas A&M University—later published *Building Profit Through Building People: Making Your Workforce the Strongest Link in the Value-Profit Chain.* In the book, Wright and his co-author Ken Carrig outline how organizations link employee engagement and workforce strength to overall profitability by applying a value-profit chain perspective. Their book points out that sustained organizational performance is driven by how effectively a company manages, develops, and leverages its people—not by short-term cost cutting or isolated HR programs.

Wright and Carrig argue that companies create competitive advantage when they treat people as strategic assets, designing integrated HR practices—selection, training, rewards, leadership, and culture—that reinforce one another and align directly with the business strategy. When an organization's practices operate in harmony, it results in improved productivity, increased dedication, and in the end, enhanced profitability.

The authors go on to provide practical guidance for HR professionals and company leaders on how investing in people—through strategic HR practices and meaningful engagement—drives customer satisfaction and ultimately financial performance, using examples from such companies as Sysco and Continental Airlines.

More recently, leadership thinker and author Simon Sinek reiterated the point in his book *Leaders Eat Last* when he wrote, "Customers will never love a company until the employees love it first."

Always start with the staff. If employees feel valued, they will in turn produce better service for the customers.

Space Center Houston's Improvements

To fulfill HR's responsibility to steward the culture and take care of employees at Spacer Center Houston, we focused on increasing leadership capacities of our management team. We pursued this strategy because research shows that nearly two-thirds of employee engagement results are directly attributable to the effectiveness of its leaders.

Specifically, Space Center Houston:

- Invested in virtual coaching for managers to provide customized development solutions that improved leadership effectiveness.
- Initiated a cross-department mentoring program for all managers, focused on enhancing relationships beyond functions and improving skills in leading people, leading change, and building coalitions.

In my early conversations with managers, many recalled previous extensive onboarding programs, both at Space

Center Houston and with other organizations. With the influx of new talent, managers wanted a priority placed on onboarding. As a result, our HR team developed a more systematic approach to every new employee's first week along with a group program, in which new employees learned more about Space Center Houston's history, mission, purpose, and values.

Focusing on the Critical Few at Space Center Houston

To leverage my lessons from NASA, I focused on the "critical few" improvement opportunities at Space Center Houston.

At the end of my first ninety days, we launched a new employee engagement team with a variety of crew members (yes, we like to use NASA terminology for our employees) who represented the broad spectrum of talent at Space Center Houston.

Half of that team explored our desired culture and the expected behaviors that are needed to achieve it. These expected behaviors were integrated with our market brand messaging and service values to create a simple, easy-to-understand, and memorable set of expectations.

The other half of the team identified perquisites (or "perks") that helped with recruitment, retention, and increased employee engagement. For each idea, team members developed business cases for presentation to leadership. Some ideas moved forward, and leaders incorporated them into their budget plans. Others did not, but team members understood from their presentations to executive leadership where their business cases fell short.

To address one of the most significant concerns across the organization, crew members first wanted improved time off flexibilities for mental health and parental or family leave. It was clear that our traditional vacation and sick leave policies needed to change. The team proposed a new paid time off approach that merged time off for vacations, sickness, and floating holidays. The approach was implemented immediately the following calendar year.

Second, crew members recommended a program for tuition reimbursement, tuition assistance, and training for other languages (Spanish or American Sign Language). While the business case did not support those programs, their proposals led to a revision to our training policy that allows reimbursements for any job or career-related training, based on department-level policies and budgets.

Third, our non-exempt staff wanted similar flexibility for remote work (one day per week) that our exempt staff enjoyed. The team developed a remote work policy framework that enabled non-exempt staff to work remotely while Space Center Houston met its legal obligation to validate actual hours worked for non-exempt staff. The policy was implemented the following calendar year.

Fourth, our crew members requested reimbursements for gym memberships. As the business case came together, the team ultimately expanded the proposal to the physical health reimbursement plan, covering not only gym memberships but also purchases for health equipment or anything that improved physical health. This was also implemented the following year.

To enhance cross-department collaboration and learning, we delivered our first-ever all-crew mentoring opportunity in 2023 with more than 40 crew members participating in nearly 150 collaborative sessions. At the completion of the program, 90 percent reported they would recommend it to others.

Throughout the process, we continued to emphasize our core values—at Space Center Houston, we are people-driven space enthusiasts who are champions of curiosity in all that we do.

Just as I learned at NASA, focusing on the "critical few" improvement opportunities at Space Center Houston significantly impacted employee engagement and organization culture. Additionally, engaging employees in developing business plans for solutions provided unique leadership development opportunities for our crew members.

New Methods of Measurement

The world of culture measurement is evolving quickly. Now, more than ever, it is important to continuously monitor and measure culture. Traditional surveys are built for gathering data. As a result, many companies are sitting on a mountain of survey data, but they still do not have a full picture of their organizations.

Today, there is a need to move beyond data collection to people connection. Employees need opportunities to express how they feel—in tone, in nuance, and in emotion. One way to do that is to conduct "stay interviews" with new employees after their first ninety days to understand what is working, what is not, and what will keep the employees engaged and committed. Unlike exit interviews—which are too late—stay interviews are proactive.

Stay interviews:

- Confirm early fit with the job, team, and culture.
- Identify friction points (training gaps, unclear expectations, workload issues).
- Reinforce what is going well to encourage retention.
- Build trust through personal, two-way conversation.
- Prevent early turnover, which is highest within the first six months.

Here are some sample questions:

- What has been your best day at work so far?
- What is one thing that has surprised you about the role or the team?
- Do you feel your skills are being used well?

- What is something that is unclear or more difficult than you expected?
- What should I be doing more or less of as your manager?
- Do you feel that any training or information is missing?
- What might cause you to look for another job?
- What do you need to feel successful and supported in the next ninety days?

Like regularly conducted stay interviews, pulse surveys (shorter surveys conducted more frequently) are becoming more popular. Additionally, with the advent of artificial intelligence (AI), there are ways to passively monitor organizational communications and get a glimpse of the culture. For example, AI tools can analyze patterns in internal emails, chat messages, or collaboration platforms to identify how often teams share feedback, recognize achievements, or escalate issues, offering a real-time snapshot of engagement, collaboration, and overall organizational culture.

Traditional feedback tools measure what people say. Now more than ever, leaders need to understand what people feel—and act on it. This can be done in a variety of ways, including using quantitative and qualitative data from surveys, focus groups, and listening sessions.

As the world continues to evolve with AI, organization leaders need to make sure they are in tune with state-of-the-art developments in culture measurement. The future belongs to leaders who turn feedback into action.

Key NASA Principle: Assess and Adapt

To create change, you must assess the culture, measure its effectiveness, and then develop the right strategies. Measuring culture can help identify the key aspects of the organization that need attention (or "the critical few")—and how the environment is either supporting or hindering your strategy.

At NASA, we asked ourselves some important reflection questions. I encourage you to do the same.

Questions for Reflection:

- How are you measuring your organization's culture?
- What barriers exist that may prevent your employees from sharing honest feedback?
- Are you clear about the critical few areas of improvement that will make the most difference?
- Are there specific groups or departments in your organization that require tailored approaches to culture improvements?
- How are you tracking progress over time and communicating changes to the organization?

As we reflected on these questions, our team moved into action. Consider the following action steps in your own journey.

Action Steps:

- Use such tools as cultural audits, employee engagement surveys, and performance metrics.
- Identify the gaps and opportunities for growth based on the data.
- Conduct regular focus groups or listening sessions to gather qualitative insights from employees, and compare those with the quantitative data from your surveys.
- Focus on the "critical few" elements that have the most significant impact on the organization's mission (e.g., communication, decision-making, or problem-solving).
- Establish cross-functional teams of employees to identify solutions, develop business cases, and share best practices to improve your organization's "critical few."
- Set measurable short-term and long-term goals for cultural improvement and celebrate milestones.
- Implement transparent communication channels to share cultural goals, progress, and challenges.

On-Orbit

The space shuttle was a winged spacecraft that carried people and cargo into and out of Earth's orbit.

Features

- Crew and cargo: The space shuttle carried up to seven astronauts and a payload.
- Thermal insulation: The space shuttle used a reusable thermal insulation system composed of ceramic tiles that were made from carbon fiber and reinforced with carbon matrix.
- Cargo bay: The space shuttle had a large bay for carrying freight, including satellites and space station components into space.
- Rocket propulsion: The space shuttle had an onboard propulsion system that used propellant to change its orbit and perform different maneuvers.

Missions

The space shuttle:

- Docked with space stations.
- Deployed satellites.
- Rendezvoused with and repaired the Hubble Space Telescope.
- Carried large parts into space to build the International Space Station.

- Conducted scientific investigations and technology demonstrations.
- Performed on-orbit repair and maintenance of satellites.

History

The space shuttle was developed by NASA and first launched in 1981. After 133 successful missions spanning 30 years, the space shuttle landed its final flight in 2011.

Organization leaders are like the space shuttle in that they carry their teams to fulfill the mission. To do so, leaders need to provide the physical, intellectual, and emotional space for their teams to accomplish their goals.

S: Strengthen Leadership and Systems

Engage leadership to model and drive cultural change.

IT STARTS WITH LEADERS. The most influential factor in any organization is the leadership team's actions, values, and decision-making processes.

As we move to the "On-Orbit" phase of building culture, it is time to focus on leaders. Culture is created by what leaders do when it is hard, not by what they say when it is easy.

An Inflection Point in My Own Leadership

Several years ago, I had an opportunity to impact and change the culture of the JSC workforce. Shortly before I became deputy HR director, our HR leadership team was engaged in conversations about diversity and inclusion. Unfortunately, we reached an impasse regarding diversity and inclusion strategies, as the white guys like me (nearly one-third of our leadership team) shut down and became silent during the conversation.

Following this meeting, I visited with Natalie Saiz, our HR director, who is a Hispanic woman. Together, we agreed a different approach to addressing diversity and inclusion was needed. We faced the challenge of engaging our entire leadership team to foster an inclusive culture aligned with JSC's long-term interests. Unfortunately, traditional methods did not work.

Due to our benchmarking efforts, I was able to connect and confer with multiple high-performing organizations, and two large private industry organizations recommended the same consultant who helped create inclusive work environments.

Natalie and I participated in the consultant's workshop examining organizational culture and its influence on diversity and inclusion initiatives. Our aim was to gain insight into how these factors affected JSC and, in turn, how our organization interacts with its broader environment. Thereafter, I sought other local opportunities to enhance my learning.

With my newfound knowledge, I shared new insights with my HR team and peers through numerous one-on-one discussions on how to build competency in diversity and inclusion. Since many in the workforce, like me, are introverted, I led book discussions covering such books as Susan Cain's *Quiet: The Power of Introverts in a World That Can't Stop Talking* and Dr. Jennifer Kahnweiler's *Quiet Influence: The Introvert's Guide to Making a Difference*. These discussions encouraged new ideas and empowered employees. Next, I initiated dialogue sessions about inclusive leadership starting with the HR team and our center director and his staff. Simultaneously, I provided opportunities for the organization to learn and engage through an extensive education strategy for our executives, managers, and supervisors that illustrated the link between inclusion and innovation. For each of these education sessions, I co-presented a "Reason Why for Inclusion and Innovation" briefing to help participants understand JSC's historical perspective and potential inclusion challenges.

Participants eagerly requested follow-up from the education sessions, so my HR team and I designed inclusion and innovation discussion groups that I co-facilitated for a dozen of JSC's top senior executives. These efforts helped many leaders engage differently and understand perspectives of employees who were different from them.

Finally, to model the building of an inclusive work environment, I filled openings in my own leadership team—starting with my deputy—by selecting people who are different from me in a variety of dimensions that included not only race and gender but also personality, style, and strengths. I wanted to surround myself with people who held different perspectives and could respectfully disagree with me if they thought I was leading the team in the wrong direction.

As we worked to improve the culture of JSC, we continued to benchmark with leading organizations. We initiated conversations with Southwest Airlines, which was widely regarded as *the* benchmark for strong organizational culture, frequently cited in business school case studies and Fortune's "Best Companies to Work For" lists.

Interestingly, Southwest Airlines was also seeking to improve their own culture, and they adopted JSC's inclusion and innovation (I&I) branding for their own efforts. Together we convened an I&I summit for executives and managers hosted at JSC. In fact, Colleen Barrett—who is best known as one of the most influential culture leaders in modern business and serving as the president of Southwest Airlines—visited JSC and gave a keynote presentation to our workforce, focusing on the principles of the airline's people-first philosophy.

Ultimately, at JSC, we realized that not being transparent about promotions negatively affected how engaged employees felt. As a result, we re-examined how key assignments and promotions were awarded and moved from a system in which less than half of promotion opportunities were awarded competitively to competing 99 percent of our promotion opportunities. In just five years, we engaged everyone in our I&I dialogue and initiatives in a variety of ways and noted how our organization's leadership illustrated the link from inclusion to innovation.

Improving Leadership Development at JSC

With the increased emphasis on this new culture strategy, engagement teams composed of employees and contractors convened to develop new approaches to improve inclusion and innovation across JSC.

The teams identified several barriers, including:

- Lack of trust.
- One-way (downward) communication.
- Lack of real-time feedback.
- Miscommunication and misconceptions.
- Different cultures and languages.

Similarly, the teams identified multiple pathways to foster inclusion and innovation, including training on servant leadership. Noting that "managers work for their people—not the other way around," the teams suggested selecting managers not only for their technical expertise but also for their servant leadership traits of trust, collegiality, accountability, authenticity, and openness.

Additionally, the teams encouraged the use of exemplars from established leadership development curricula focused on building trust, enhancing engagement, advancing innovation, and leading high-performing teams.

Following those recommendations, I took the lead on an effort to refresh, update, and improve our leadership curricula at JSC with an internal advisory group.

Our benchmarking revealed that the best companies for leadership development shared several key traits. The companies:

- Invested time and money in developing leaders.
- Identified promising leaders early.
- Chose assignments strategically.
- Developed leaders within their current jobs.
- Provided feedback and support.
- Developed teams, not just individuals.
- Exerted leadership through inspiration.
- Made leadership a key component of the organization's culture.

Key factors for successful leadership development practices included:

S: STRENGTHEN LEADERSHIP AND SYSTEMS

- An external focus that defines success in terms of customers and stakeholders.
- Clear thinking, imagination, and courage.
- Deep domain expertise—before pursuing breadth.
- Inclusive behavior, building relationships, and making connections.

Additionally, leading organizations leverage training strategically. First, training is part of their strategy to drive culture change—courses aren't just classes; they serve as a critical strategy to advance the new culture. Second, training is steadily paced with one key focus area each year. Third, training is about building capacity because you cannot hold people accountable until they have the skills and capacity to perform.

Through our benchmarking, we recognized that our leadership needed to be more consistent in the leadership behaviors they emphasized. Instead of continually recognizing technical results, a more balanced approach was needed for people leadership. Unfortunately, for many leaders, developing people was an afterthought, and individual development plans (IDPs) were nothing more than a "check the box" activity.

The training strategy needed to work hand-in-hand with how leaders were recognized and held accountable, and senior leaders needed to ensure the right leadership behaviors and principles were understood and reinforced.

My internal advisory group took this information, and we:

- Simplified the JSC leadership model (aligning with the core competencies of leading change, leading people, being results driven, having business acumen, and building coalitions).
- Defined core courses for leaders at all levels.
- Added a foundations of leadership class for individual contributors and influence leaders.
- Required a course on giving and receiving feedback for supervisors and team leaders.
- Outlined a strategy to accelerate leadership transitions from lead to supervisor; from supervisor to manager; and from manager to executive.

Research backed up our approach. A leadership excellence survey of over 1,000 organizations recognized that top organizations promoted continuous learning at all levels of the organization. Their report noted that all successful organizations accomplish their missions through effective leadership, especially in rapidly changing environments.

Top organizations also adopted a values-based, transformational leadership model that retained their core values, honored past successes, and established strategic priorities to meet future challenges. Their extensive leadership training frameworks allowed leaders the opportunity to learn foundational leadership concepts and core values.

S: STRENGTHEN LEADERSHIP AND SYSTEMS

According to Bersin & Associates, "Our research over the last five years clearly shows that high-performing organizations take leadership very seriously. Top performing companies in every industry segment are led by individuals with deep levels of experience and understanding of the business, comprehensive abilities to see the future and drive change, and a unique set of personal skills that fit into the culture of their organization. Such a complex set of capabilities takes years to develop and must be continuously improved. Excellent business leaders are like athletes—they continually work on their game."

When the U.S. Nuclear Regulatory Commission made the leap to the Best Place to Work in the Federal Government in 2009, they noted how the mission and values reflected in their strategic plan were widely understood and embraced by staff. Additional keys to their success included:

- Management styles and valuing differences among employees were close to best-in-class levels.
- Management supported innovative solutions and highly valued individual input.
- All employees demonstrated strong respect and cooperation.
- There were extensive opportunities for personal and professional growth.
- Employees were comfortable in expressing differing views with management.

- Employees were fulfilled and considered their jobs important.

At NRC, inclusion was a key theme—it was clear they valued diversity of thought and ideas, encouraging a collaborative work environment. They worked to align the organization's mission, vision, and values with the people.

NRC leaders emphasized continuous learning. In fact, as previously noted, their goal was to have 70 percent of staff complete at least 24 hours of training per year. Then, they strongly encouraged development plans for individuals and executives alike. All new employees were assigned coaches and mentors during their first two years.

Common Themes for Success

From research and benchmarking, JSC's internal advisory group identified the following criteria for success:

Align Leadership Principles and Philosophy with Criteria for Selection, Training, and Accountability

Leading organizations articulate a set of leadership principles and create a shared understanding among their leaders and managers about these principles (they explain the "why"). These principles then serve as a guiding light for all organization decisions.

High-performing organizations also align selection and performance management practices with desired leadership styles and philosophy. Then they consistently implement and execute, creating a culture of accountability.

Use a Simple Leadership Model

Our team determined that the NASA leadership model was too complex and not well-understood by senior leaders. As an alternative, the core competencies used across the federal government for selection and performance management were well understood. So we moved to align NASA's feedback reports for leaders with:

- Achieving results
- Leading change
- Leading people
- Attaining business acumen
- Building coalitions

Create a Roadmap for Leadership Curricula Customized by Leader Level

JSC's previous approach to leadership training was to offer an extensive menu of options that could be customized to meet an individual's development needs. Following the team's benchmarking and research, it became clear that we needed to be more prescriptive in our approach to the leadership curricula to ensure a core body of knowledge at each leadership level.

Individual contributors and influence leaders took a foundations of leadership course, an introduction to inclusion and innovation, and a course on giving and receiving feedback.

Group and team leaders took a seminar in leadership, an inclusion and innovation workshop, a giving and receiving performance-enhancing feedback course, and monthly sessions of management tips.

Front-line supervisors took a seminar in management, the inclusion and innovation workshop, a management for supervisors course, a course on developing people, and a course on giving and receiving performance-enhancing feedback.

Executives were encouraged to pursue continuous learning through executive education offerings outside of NASA.

The goal of the training strategy was to offer training before it was needed. To do so, we had to commit to investments in our workforce by growing leaders early in their leadership journey. We wanted to provide timely training to meet the needs of new leaders and leadership transitions and to support the needs of non-supervisory group and team leaders.

We then asked ourselves how we were driving accountability for people leadership. At the time, evaluations of executives were based 60 percent on technical results and 40 percent on leadership competencies. It was clear through this approach that we heavily valued technical expertise and results.

We wanted to bring an increased emphasis on the importance of people leadership. To that end, we moved to a model where executive bonuses were based on a balance of technical achievements (50 percent) and how those results were achieved (50 percent). Evaluators needed to determine if their executive's methods were consistent with the desired leadership behaviors and principles. The results were remarkable, as productivity remained high while employee engagement continued to soar, as people leadership was seen as its own technical discipline.

Building Coaching Skills

As we moved forward, we recognized that coaching skills were crucial for leaders for our strategy of inclusion and innovation to succeed.

Frankly, NASA had quite the journey with coaching, not unlike many organizations. For me, history always provides a good frame of reference. In 1848, the term "coach" was first used as university slang for a personal private tutor. It was based on the metaphor that to move from one point to another swiftly, you would ride on a horse-drawn coach, which would require the help of a coachman. By 1861, the term was applied to athletics.

Fundamentally, the goal or outcome of coaching is to facilitate a change or transformation. The International

Coach Federation, which certifies coaches, says coaching is partnering with clients in a thought-provoking and creative process that inspires them to maximize their personal and professional potential.

NASA always seeks to make the complex simple. The agency says a coach helps you achieve your goals to get from where you are (for us, it is on Earth) to where you want to be (the moon or Mars).

Coaches assist others in ways that set them apart from other kinds of organizational helpers. First, consultants advise based on their professional expertise. They often lend their expertise to specific challenges.

Second, counselors focus on personal, existing issues typically related to emotions, attitudes, or behaviors. NASA—like many organizations—offered an employee assistance program composed of trained counselors who focused on employee mental health and wellness.

Third, mentors advise and impart wisdom based on personal experiences. Mentoring has a long history at JSC. Over many years, participation among its 3,000 employees declined from 500 to 200. As a result, a group of employees recommended a new mentoring program. They named it YODA ("Your Opportunity to Develop Another"). JSC even secured branding rights with LucasFilms, who designed and produced custom-made Yoda pins to recognize mentors.

S: STRENGTHEN LEADERSHIP AND SYSTEMS

For the program's kickoff and graduation events, we used *Star Wars* characters, and I even dressed as Darth Vader (my boys thought I had the coolest job)! The program was a success, drawing 750 employees (or 25 percent of the overall population).

As we continued to research state-of-the-art mentoring programs, we learned about the importance of reverse and two-way mentoring. As a result, we had to move away from the Yoda branding to the JSC Formal Mentoring Program—a much less exciting brand but a more effective program.

The JSC Formal Mentoring Program incorporated other events beyond just one-on-one matching, including "Speed Mentoring" events that engaged 200 to 300 participants each quarter. For these events, we used tables of eight (two mentors with six participants) and offered questions for table discussion. Then we rotated participants, so they would receive mentoring from at least ten mentors over a ninety-minute period. It was a great way to get more people involved who were not already part of a formal mentoring engagement.

Incidentally, the lesson of two-way mentoring has stuck with me. Over the last three years at Space Center Houston, we started with thirty managers and leaders in cross-department mentoring relationships. Then, we convened our first open mentoring program with 25 percent of employees participating. Most recently, we assigned thirty-five pairs of "co-mentors," representing 35 percent of our overall population. During that cycle, I appreciated a reverse mentoring relationship with one of our education instructors, and we discussed the effectiveness of HR policies and workforce communications.

A fourth organization role that differs from mentors is that of managers, who focus on individual and organizational goals. One of the most influential executive coaches in the world, Marshall Goldsmith, encourages managers to focus on "feed forward"—performance-enhancing feedback focused on the future.

NASA's first quarter-century was heavily influenced by the Department of Defense. The predominant leadership style incorporated yelling at, and in some cases demeaning, technical experts to ensure they really knew and were sure of what they were talking about—with little room for error.

By the 1990s when I joined the organization, NASA was moving to a different organization culture and leadership style. However, many leaders had been promoted and rewarded for a brash leadership style. So, in the late-1990s and early 2000s, NASA would bring in outside coaches to correct performance or behavior deficiencies. For example, some managers engaged in personal attacks or threw "tantrums" and were assigned a coach. Fortunately, such behavior is no longer tolerated.

S: STRENGTHEN LEADERSHIP AND SYSTEMS

Launching Leaders—Strategically

In my early days, if problems or issues arose, one response was "you need a coach." So early on, coaching had a negative connotation.

Following Michael Watkins' publication of *The First 90 Days* and his follow-up titled *The First 90 Days in Government*, NASA began to see the value of coaches in helping leaders make transitions. As you might imagine, some leaders were resistant because of the stigma around the use of external coaches (that NASA itself created).

Notwithstanding the stigma, NASA brought in external coaches to help accelerate transitions for new supervisors or new mid-level managers (manager of manager roles) and leveraged external coaches as part of NASA's leadership development programs.

In fact, when coaching was used as part of leadership transitions, NASA would brand it as a "Strategic Leader Launch." As a result, some leaders began to embrace coaching as a tool. The tide turned into a more strategic focus and intentional investment in engagements with external coaches.

In more recent years, NASA consistently used external coaches to build leaders. The agency saw it as an investment in leadership development, so strategic choices were made about those investments. The era of remedial coaching had ended, since many behaviors once accepted were now considered unacceptable.

Many leaders received professional coaching and reported its value to their colleagues. This moved the perception of coaching from a negative to a positive one.

Then came budget cuts. NASA's training budget, which had been increased for post–space shuttle retirement, was cut nearly in half, so we had to start thinking differently about doing more with less for training and development. Many of our external coaching engagements were expensive, and we could no longer afford the internal coaching certification programs for our HR professionals.

So we needed to fundamentally revisit the question of "Who is a coach?"

My wife is a big Tom Landry fan, and he once said, "A coach is someone who gets you to do what you don't want to do, so you can be who you want to be." That quote resonates for me since my wife is a coach, and she can often get me to do what I don't want to do.

Similarly, as former U.S. First Lady Rosalynn Carter put it, "A manager takes people where they want to go. A great leader takes people where they don't necessarily want to go, but ought to be."

What if we started thinking differently here? Can we replace the word "coach" with the word "leader"?

S: STRENGTHEN LEADERSHIP AND SYSTEMS

A leader helps others achieve a specific goal. A leader is change-oriented and forward-looking.

At NASA, we believed coaching was a learnable skill that could be taught, practiced, and honed for everyone. In true NASA fashion, we came up with an acronym. "LET'S TALK" is a tool to help us remember how to coach and then how to recognize good coaching.

The first four letters in the LET'S TALK acronym, or the LET'S, outline the steps of coaching—the how-to:

- Listen
- Engage
- Trust
- Synergize

Listen

The first thing to do as a coach is to listen. Listen without the intent to respond. Don't talk. Really listen to what people are saying, but most importantly, what they mean. Listening, like coaching, is a skill that needs to be practiced.

Leaders at all levels need to practice active listening. Some tactics to practice active listening include:

- *Paraphrase*: Reflect on what the person said, internally and externally. Rephrase and restate what the person said using different words to achieve clarity, to make sure your understanding is a true

representation of what was meant to be said. For example, you can start by saying "What I hear you saying is ___."
- *Reflect*: Most people find it annoying if you repeat word for word what they just said. Instead, reflect internally on what the speaker said. It is okay to ask them to repeat something you may have missed, especially if the conversation has a technical component. For example, "Could you repeat…?"
- *Probe*: Ask follow-up questions to gain greater insight and clarity. Avoid close-ended or yes/no questions. Instead, ask open-ended questions. Avoid leading questions or those with embedded assumptions. For example, instead of "Did that make you feel appreciated?" you could ask, "How did that make you feel?"
- *Clarify*: Similar to paraphrasing, clarify by offering to the speaker the essential meaning or a summary of what they just said. Also, offer clarification of any coaching advice you may have given. The purpose of clarification is for both parties to come to a consensus about what is being said. For example, "Let's see if I'm clear about this … am I understanding the situation fully?"

There is some overlap in these listening tactics, and not all of them should be used in every coaching conversation. But these are some tools to keep in mind when you are in a coaching conversation.

S: STRENGTHEN LEADERSHIP AND SYSTEMS

Engage

As a coach, you need to engage with people. Get to know them, not just what they do. Really getting to know people requires another coaching skill that NASA developed in its technical leaders—namely, emotional intelligence, which encourages leaders to understand the differences in communication styles as well as their own personality quirks. This was often done through personality assessments (e.g., Meyers-Briggs, the Birkman, DiSC, StrengthsFinder, or the Change Style Indicator). Some of these assessments are publicly available and can be easily administered and interpreted.

Learning about people and understanding their differences allows leaders to go beyond the Golden Rule, which says to treat others the way *you* want to be treated. The Platinum Rule says to treat others the way *they* want to be treated. The Platinum Rule teaches that respect and results come from empathy in action—the disciplined practice of understanding others and flexing your style to meet their needs. It reframes leadership as a relational skill rather than a positional one.

One former head of NASA (the self-described "Chief Engineer of the Universe") used to say, "I don't do feelings." We needed to change that for effective leadership.

Why are feelings hard to talk about? What makes it hard to talk about them? How can you watch the feelings of your team members and engage with them differently?

Trust

Moving on to the first "T" in the LET'S TALK acronym is the notion of trust. A coach works to build trust. Stephen Covey's *Speed of Trust* breaks down trust into two main components: competency and character.

Competency generally speaks of a person's capability, the technical breadth and depth they possess. You are more likely to trust a brain surgeon who has completed medical school than one who has not—a very sensible component of trust.

The other component of trust is credibility, or the person's character or sometimes their reputation. I love my wife; she is very credible in my eyes—I trust her with our kids, our checkbook, and key life decisions, but I would not recommend her as my brain surgeon because that is not her competency. By the way, she would rightfully say the same about me.

Synergize

As a coach, remember you are not "telling." In fact, good leaders and coaches do not give answers; they ask questions. Synergize simply means "two heads are better than one." Remember, your goal is to help someone get from where they are to where they want to be. It may be the case that you need to give an individual more directed, assertive advice. But really, a coach is someone who gets you to the answer you already knew. At best, it is a creative

S: STRENGTHEN LEADERSHIP AND SYSTEMS

collaboration. The person you are coaching is also an expert. They have the best insight into their own situation and their own life goals. Therefore, work together to form a solution.

Going further, if you start to think about the steps in coaching as integrated steps, "synergize" takes on a deeper meaning. Combining what we learned about engaging people with different personalities, synergize means we embrace differences as we work towards a solution. Stephen Covey says in *The 7 Habits of Highly Effective People* that "the essence of synergy is to value differences—to respect them, to build on strengths, to compensate for weaknesses."

As a recap, here are the steps of coaching (LET'S):

- Listen first.
- Engage with people, understanding their differences.
- Trust others.
- Synergize or work together to form a solution.

Moving from the steps of coaching, we should explore what good, effective coaching looks like. What are the characteristics of coaching we need to instill in leaders?

The last four letters focus on the aspects of coaching, or what the "TALK" should be:

- Timely
- Affirming
- Lateral
- Kinetic

Timely

First, coaching is timely. It is constant communication. It is not simply a check-the-box sort of activity. Millennials and Generation Z employees want more coaching. Nearly 80 percent say they want their supervisors to provide coaching. They are used to instant feedback and a give-and-take relationship.

Coaching occurs in the moment. It is timely in that it needs to occur within an appropriate response time, if it is dealing with a situational circumstance. A leader is not concerned with coaching only during a performance review cycle.

A good leader is always concerned with coaching people. At the same time, a coaching conversation should occur at an appropriate time, considering the personality aspects of the person receiving the coaching. An introvert may need extra time to process a particular circumstance, while an extrovert may welcome "hashing things out" immediately.

Affirming

Coaching is positive. As mentioned before, coaching once had a connotation of correction. NASA and other organizations are turning the negative perceptions about coaching around to something positive. So good coaching should provide encouragement. Good leaders are supportive of their people, like good coaches.

NASA used appreciative inquiry as a technique. In the words of Thomas H. White, former head of GTE Telephone Operations, "Appreciative inquiry focuses us on the positive aspects of our lives and leverages them to correct the negative. It's the opposite of 'problem-solving.'" A fundamental assumption of appreciative inquiry is that systems grow in the direction of the questions they ask.

Here are some examples of appreciative inquiry: "What positive legacy do you hope to leave behind when you move on from your current role in the organization?" "How would you like to make your position better than it was when you first started?"

Lateral

Moving on to the "L" in the TALK portion of our LET'S TALK acronym, coaching is a lateral activity. It is reciprocal in that it provides an opportunity for growth on both sides of the conversation. This often happens implicitly, unbeknownst to the person receiving the coaching, but leaders learn from their people as much as they do from their own leaders and mentors.

Interestingly, NASA encouraged reverse mentoring in its formal mentoring program at JSC. Part of the reason for reverse mentoring is to bridge generational gaps, but it is also to promote the idea of continued learning throughout the leadership journey. Coaching gives an opportunity for leaders to increase their self-awareness and reflect on their communication styles, goals and aspirations, and how they can approach challenges in new ways.

Kinetic

Finally, the last letter in our LET'S TALK acronym really sums up the overall spirit of coaching. The K is for kinetic, meaning that coaching is dynamic. Taking the time to coach someone should energize them—it should create a positive energy for personal growth.

From InsideOut Coaching, based on Alan Fine's book *You Already Know How to be Great*, this kinetic aspect of coaching is called "fire." The idea is that it takes fire, or positive energy, to take our focus on the goal ahead, to combine it with a faith that we can achieve, and to really get from where we are to where we want to be.

To review the aspects of coaching, good, effective coaching is:

- *Timely*: It occurs in the moment.
- *Affirming*: It is a positive experience.
- *Lateral*: It provides opportunities for growth on both sides.
- *Kinetic*: It gives energy and the fire needed to achieve.

Which coaching skill should you prioritize for your own professional development? What specific action will you take this week to enhance that skill? How will you evaluate your progress and determine success? Who will be responsible for supporting your accountability in achieving this goal?

Growing Out-of-This-World Leaders

For many years, NASA ranked best in the U.S. government for effective leadership, and the Johnson Space Center even topped NASA's overall score among all field centers.

As previously noted, NASA's talent strategy led to nearly 95 percent internal promotions up to and through the executive ranks by fostering a development mindset for all.

NASA intentionally identified a pool of talent for future senior leadership roles, providing focused assessments and strategic individual development plans.

Leaders strongly focused on leading change in a VUCA (volatile, uncertain, complex, and ambiguous) world and emphasized leading people and supervision as a separate but equally important technical discipline. That mindset helped leaders understand the criticality of leading people to their own success.

For developmental purposes, NASA referenced the "70/20/10 model," originally proposed by the Center for Creative Leadership. This framework asserts that the majority of leadership development occurs through practical, real-world experience, while interpersonal relationships and formal education contribute supplementary value. Specifically, 70 percent of a leader's growth stems from on-the-job experiences and challenges; 20 percent originates from interactions with others—such as mentors, coaches, and colleagues who provide constructive feedback; and 10 percent derives from formal courses or training programs.

70% Context (Job/Projects/Tasks)

NASA emphasized progressively more responsible roles for leaders. My NASA career provided a prime example of this, as I steadily moved from group lead to deputy supervisor. Then I was promoted to my first front-line supervisory position before I became a manager of managers. I was then ready to step into an HR executive role before supervising other HR executives and ultimately becoming NASA's deputy chief human capital officer.

During my career, I was also afforded developmental assignments at NASA Headquarters, outside of NASA—to the World Bank's International Finance Corporation, and outside of HR as a front-line leader for engineering at JSC.

Each of these job rotations was intentionally and strategically managed. JSC used a rotation and mobility board to select leaders for key assignments and then managed their re-entry plans following job rotations to take full advantage of the investment.

To enhance leadership development, JSC executives organized round-table discussions to evaluate the performance and potential of emerging leaders. The conversations centered on offering recommendations for cultivating talent at the next leadership level.

At Space Center Houston, we recently used a similar approach to conduct our own succession development conversation, providing feedback from executives to all director-level staff. We chose to provide feedback to everyone at the next level—not just a select few of "high potentials," recognizing that everyone can grow and improve if given the opportunity to do so.

20% Contacts (Coaching/Mentoring/Shadowing)

The next part of the strategy involves learning from other people—mentors, coaches, and observations of other leaders. NASA leveraged both formal and informal mentoring and encouraged two-way mentoring relationships as well as reverse mentoring.

As you consider your own development, I like to ask leaders, "Who is on your Mount Rushmore of mentors?" If you cannot quickly identify multiple people who have shaped your own leadership, you need to seek a mentor today.

NASA also emphasized the importance of networking and building relationships with leaders across the organization, especially since teamwork is a core value, critical to the success of human space flight.

10% Concepts (Training/Development/Reading)

The last part of the leadership development focuses on the content. This is generally the first thing on leaders' minds when they consider leadership development: "What course should I take?" or "What conference should I attend?"

While these are important to developing leaders, I agree they only provide about 10 percent of the impact. As you will recall, NASA developed leadership curricula to ensure systematic learning, as outlined previously.

A Case Study in Applying Lessons from NASA

While I have spoken at several international conferences over the years about "Growing Out-of-This-World Leaders" (or "Building Leaders the NASA Way"), I had the opportunity to prove these concepts at Space Center Houston. Unlike NASA's 18,000-employee workforce, Space Center Houston has 200 full-time with another 250 part-time and seasonal staff with about 30 people leaders.

S: STRENGTHEN LEADERSHIP AND SYSTEMS

At Space Center Houston, our talent strategy shifted from less than 10 percent internal promotions to a commitment that we would fill half of our new roles with internal talent.

We applied NASA's framework for succession development, reaching a common understanding about pools of talent available to meet SCH's needs. Additionally, we used a process for purposeful development for future leaders, which sets the stage for even more meaningful individual development plans.

Our philosophy and methodology promote a culture of continuous development while incorporating executive insights regarding the next generation of leaders. Executive coach extraordinaire Marshall Goldsmith says, "Great leaders encourage development by openly developing themselves."

At Space Center Houston, we started with some quick wins aligned with the "20% Contacts" strategy. We brought BetterUp's virtual coaching program that was used at NASA to all people leaders. Each leader embraced the opportunity, engaging in nearly two coaching sessions each per month.

We measured the effectiveness of different aspects of the coaching program. In one measure of psychological safety—the extent to which people feel they can take risks, voice thoughts and concerns without fear of retribution, and freely ask for help without fear of judgment—the results were remarkable, showing a 34 percent improvement.

As we are now learning through neuroscience research and biological realities, leaders who enhance trust, safety, and belonging improve engagement across their teams.

We also started a cross-department mentoring program that included twenty pairs of managers for the organization and enhanced relationships that were critical for organization growth.

For the "10% Concepts," Space Center Houston already had its own leadership development program, provided to external clients that leveraged how NASA trains astronauts with these three mindsets:

- *Expeditionary Mindset*: Explore your leadership style.
- *Growth Mindset*: Consider the art of the possible.
- *Overview Effect*: This is the view astronauts describe of the earth from space. It changes your perspective, and you recognize that "we're in this together."

We were able to bring this leadership development program to our own staff. In 2025, we also initiated first-ever leadership cohorts, so our leaders could learn skills in basic supervision and share best practices with one another.

S: STRENGTHEN LEADERSHIP AND SYSTEMS

I am pleased to see how we are building leadership capacities at Space Center Houston, strengthening leadership and systems, as we are **Building Culture the NASA Way**.

Key NASA Principle: Strengthen Leadership and Systems

It starts with leaders. The most influential factor in any organization is the leadership team's actions, values, and decision-making processes.

As John Maxwell puts it, "Everything rises and falls on leadership." It is not what leaders say. It is what they demonstrate through their actions, consistency, and example.

Developing leaders is a systematic process—it is not just a set of workshops, but it involves a full operating rhythm.

At NASA, we asked ourselves some important reflection questions. I encourage you to do the same.

Questions for Reflection:

- What is your organization doing to develop the next generation of leaders?
- How do you identify future leaders within your organization?
- Are you conducting regular assessments of your leadership pipeline to ensure it reflects the diversity and skillsets needed for the future?
- What opportunities exist for emerging leaders to gain cross-departmental experience or mentorship?

S: STRENGTHEN LEADERSHIP AND SYSTEMS

- How are you ensuring that leadership development initiatives are accessible to a diverse range of employees?
- Are your leadership development strategies and systems aligned with the culture you seek to build?

As we reflected on these questions, our team moved into action. Consider the following action steps in your own journey.

Action Steps:

- Build systems that support leadership development and provide feedback to drive culture.
- Establish cross-functional project teams to give emerging leaders hands-on experience in collaborative environments.
- Implement regular leadership forums or roundtables to share best practices and lessons learned across departments.
- Develop mentorship and sponsorship programs that connect senior leaders with early-career talent.
- Integrate inclusivity and innovation into leadership evaluations and development.
- Conduct periodic reviews of leadership development programs to ensure alignment with evolving organizational culture and strategic priorities.
- Provide training for leaders on inclusive decision-making and psychological safety to reinforce a culture in which all voices are valued.

Re-Entry

THE SPACE SHUTTLE'S RE-ENTRY into Earth's atmosphere was a hypersonic glide at high speeds and temperatures.

The shuttle re-entered at speeds of about 17,000 miles per hour, which generated significant heat.

The air temperature near the shuttle's leading edge reached as high as 3,000°F, and the heat produced by re-entry was so great that it could melt most materials. The shuttle's thermal protection system included heat-resistant tiles that were critical to protecting the shuttle and its crew.

The shuttle used a special high angle of attack to generate drag and dissipate speed, as it was designed to land like a commercial airplane.

Just as the space shuttle re-entered the atmosphere, building culture can be done smoothly, even in VUCA (volatile, uncertain, complex, and ambiguous) conditions.

A: Activate Inclusion and Innovation

Build a culture that prioritizes inclusivity and innovation, while effectively communicating progress.

THE FINAL PHASE IS about activating cultural transformation by creating an environment that promotes inclusion and fosters innovation. To thrive, it is critical to build safe spaces where diverse perspectives are heard and new ideas can flourish. This is best achieved through transparent and ongoing communication.

Space shuttle re-entry was a critical phase, requiring top experts in the Mission Control Center to monitor systems and ensure a safe return.

Organizations often face VUCA (volatile, uncertain, complex, and ambiguous) conditions when building culture.

Let's take a look at some complexities faced by NASA. The average NASA employee was nearly fifty years old with twenty years of experience. Over the last thirty years, NASA's attrition rate—without special incentives, such as buyouts—held steady at around 5 percent. That meant the workforce changed very slowly over time, and less than 5 percent of NASA employees were under the age of thirty.

I once heard that it could take half of your average tenure to change your organization culture. With that guideline, it should take about ten years, crossing at least two presidential administrations. A more commonly held belief is that it can take three to five years to embed new behaviors, norms, and habits. Either way, shifting NASA's culture is a bit like turning the *Titanic*.

How Did NASA Do It?

NASA constantly pushes the boundaries of what humans believe is possible. NASA is forward leaning, always looking at new technologies and cutting-edge solutions. Every employee plays a unique role in shaping workforce identity and helping create solutions.

A: ACTIVATE INCLUSION AND INNOVATION

When we consider employee engagement and culture, NASA started with its annual survey. As noted in the Assess and Adapt section, survey results provided valuable insights.

Results generally indicated a highly motivated workforce across the entire federal government—more than 90 percent of survey respondents reported that they gave extra effort when necessary and consistently sought ways to improve, and NASA's global satisfaction beat the overall government job satisfaction by 15 percent.

Senior executives cite innovation as an important driver of growth, but few organizations really achieve a culture of innovation. While it requires focus, intention, and persistence, the specific strategies for leading and managing innovation can be applied to any organization.

The "Innovation Index": NASA's Three Key Measures

The Partnership for Public Service—which is responsible for the "Best Places to Work in the Federal Government," or the government's equivalent to Forbes' "Best Places to Work" lists—devised the "Innovation Index."

Since the index was initially developed in 2010, NASA topped the list even before it achieved the "Best Place to Work" distinction.

The Innovation Index is composed of these three questions:

1. Are you consistently looking for ways to better perform your job?
2. Do you feel encouraged to come up with new and better ways of doing things?
3. Are creativity and innovation rewarded?

As you can see, this is not rocket science. In fact, you should take the time to pause and consider how you would evaluate your current team or organization using those questions.

When we talked about culture at NASA Johnson Space Center, we used a set of expected behaviors developed by the JSC Joint Leadership Team that comprised government and contractor executives. These behaviors directly contribute to the culture of innovation and provide principles and guidelines needed for quality decision-making.

Each member of the JSC Team is accountable—professionally, technically, and fiscally—to coworkers, the team, the management, and the taxpayers. Here are JSC's expected behaviors:

- *Be Respectful*: Demonstrate consideration or appreciation. Appreciate the creativity and broader perspective of a diverse team, because diversity is vital to success.
- *Be Trustworthy*: Act with integrity and honor.
- *Be Accountable*: Be responsible for your actions.
- *Be Open-Minded*: Be receptive. Seek knowledge that will strengthen yourselves and the team. Look

A: ACTIVATE INCLUSION AND INNOVATION

for innovative ways to address challenges. Look inward for areas of improvement.
- *Be a Key Player*: Get results. All team members are engaged contributors who develop solutions.

Every year since the Partnership for Public Service's "Best Places to Work" rankings launched, effective leadership emerged as the key driver. In fact, about 60 percent of any change in survey results can be explained by the employees' perspective of their management.

A few years ago, Max Stier, president of the Partnership for Public Service, testified in front of Congress. One congressional member argued that the NASA mission certainly drives its success on the survey. Stier responded that most employees across the federal government are very supportive and are aligned with their agency missions. He noted the difference between the highest and lowest performing agencies is largely attributed to leadership—especially on the front lines.

So front-line leadership is key. That's a big reason why I left my deputy director of human resources role for a front-line management position in our Engineering Directorate. I wanted to get a front-row seat and perspective on their daily challenges and issues and walk in our front-line leaders' shoes. It was an enriching experience. It greatly enhanced my perspective when I was later promoted to my first executive role as HR director at the Johnson Space Center.

Building a Culture of Innovation

As we continue to look at how to build a culture of innovation, you will quickly see the practical approaches that we used and that this is not unique to NASA or rocket science. According to the Partnership for Public Service's research (and a meta-analysis of the government's employee engagement survey), six questions are the major drivers for the three questions of the Innovation Index. We shall explore each of them.

#1—Recognition

Driver #1 for a culture of innovation is based on the survey item "Employees are rewarded for providing high quality products and services."

In the 1960s—at the outset of NASA, the hallmark for recognition for the federal government was the United States Forest Service's Smokey Bear.

NASA sought a similar icon and turned to cartoonist Charles M. Schulz, an avid supporter of the U.S. space program. He immediately agreed to let NASA use "Snoopy the Astronaut" at no cost, and Schulz himself drew the image for NASA's unique award pin.

The resulting "Silver Snoopy Award" is the astronaut corps' unique way of recognizing less than one percent of the workforce each year. Employees are specifically recognized for improving astronauts' ability to safely do their

A: ACTIVATE INCLUSION AND INNOVATION

jobs. Past recipients include the developers of the lunar rover (also known as the "moon buggy") and life-support systems. By keeping it highly selective, the award still holds its power and meaning after sixty years!

This provided a unique start to NASA's long-standing history of robust awards programs that recognize employees' pursuit of innovative ideas. NASA's awards programs emphasize innovative achievements and celebrate exceptional long-standing service of both individuals and teams.

Have you seen the 1995 movie *Apollo 13*? It highlights the heroic efforts of mission controllers at NASA to bring astronauts—who were flying on a damaged spacecraft—safely home.

One of the lead flight directors, Gene Kranz, famously wrote a book about the experience titled *Failure Is Not an Option*. While that mindset and focus were critical to saving human lives for the 1970 mission, that same mindset ultimately permeated NASA culture. As a result, NASA was not taking generally accepted risks when developing new technologies and systems that did not affect crew safety.

So NASA had to create a new recognition program that rewarded a culture of appropriate risk-taking. As an agency, NASA needed to welcome and nurture a culture of innovation in which failure was seen as merely a steppingstone to success.

Leaders began to emphasize to NASA employees, "Whenever you encounter failure, use it as an opportunity for learning. If you are a responsible risk-taker and always strive for success, a few bumps in the road will only make you a better innovator."

Whether a specific innovation involved creating something new, improving existing technologies or processes, or adapting a tried-and-true idea to a new context, NASA encouraged leaders to promote risk-taking.

Champion of Innovation Award

Supervisors and managers play a unique role in fostering innovation at NASA. In addition to being innovative themselves, they support and encourage employees to think outside the box and become creative problem solvers.

Therefore, NASA initiated an award designed to recognize the supervisors and managers who build a culture of appropriate risk-taking and who support and encourage creative and innovative behaviors from their employees.

To receive the award, excellence was required in the following:

1. Leadership
    - Did the leader foster innovation by creating conditions that enable the team to openly contribute to and achieve objectives?

- Did the leader articulate high-performance expectations while giving individuals the ability to engage in innovative behaviors?

2. Vision

- Did the leader recognize the opportunity to make things better and formulate a new or different path forward?
- Did the leader demonstrate how he or she gathered information, input, and insights from others at every step?
- Did the leader establish challenging project goals and link them to the needs of the organization?

3. Relationship Building

- Did the leader persuade others to support and/or contribute to an idea or initiative?
- Did the leader overcome objections by using personal credibility and prior positive relationships?
- How did the leader collaboratively interact with his or her staff to support high levels of teamwork and provide opportunities to share innovations?

4. Role Modeling

- Was the leader respected and recognized by peers as someone who demonstrates creative and innovative behaviors?

- Were the actions of the leader perceived as creative by others, influencing and challenging them to question, observe, network, and experiment beyond the obvious?
- Did he or she lead by example?
- Did the leader ask questions, make suggestions, question assumptions, and challenge the status quo?

It is important to note that NASA did not place the burden for building a culture of innovation entirely on the shoulders of its leaders. Employees also were responsible for creating that culture.

Lean Forward; Fail Smart Award

Failure does not have to be negative. In fact, many technology companies—and those who require innovation to survive and thrive in competitive environments—place the highest value on failure to bring new ideas to the market.

Having the right attitude and supportive processes in place, failure can be educational, informative, and sometimes transformative.

The Lean Forward; Fail Smart Award was designed to encourage, recognize, and celebrate the spirit that propels individuals to take the risk to innovate, unfortunately failing to reach the desired outcome but learning from the attempt.

A: ACTIVATE INCLUSION AND INNOVATION

For the award, NASA used the following criteria:

1. **Dare to Try**

    - Did the effort demonstrate risk-taking behavior to achieve ground-breaking innovation?
    - Did the nominee exhibit the courage to depart from usual practice to enable new thinking to thrive?

2. **Perseverance**

    - Did the team show a determined will to succeed and a "never-give-up" attitude, even after repeated failed attempts?
    - Did the team effectively respond to unforeseen circumstances?
    - Does the effort demonstrate that failures are often inevitable steppingstones to innovation?

3. **Learning**

    - Did the team apply lessons learned after failing to achieve desired results?
    - Did the team demonstrate an ability to distinguish between productive and unproductive failures?
    - Did the team make decisions about whether to fail or scale, based on pilot and recurrent testing—in other words, did they fail smart?

4. Collaboration
   - Did the team consistently share its knowledge with others so mistakes would not be repeated?
   - Did they openly collaborate and network to gain perspectives from individuals with diverse backgrounds through building relationships, participating in teams, and partnering with others both internal and external to NASA?

One of the first winners of this new award was NASA's Project Morpheus, which was chartered to test advanced spacecraft technologies—including an uncrewed planetary lander designed for future missions to the moon, asteroids, or Mars.

Project Morpheus focused on developing a new technology that would allow spacecraft to safely navigate and land on a rocky surface without human intervention. Another objective was testing a new propulsion system.

Project Morpheus was an example of lean engineering development: it used rapid prototyping, accepted higher technical risk, and prioritized fast learning over building super-robust hardware up front. It had a very flat organizational structure, encouraged strong collaboration (both in-person and online), and used existing tools to keep things lightweight and efficient.

Project Morpheus accepted that failure (or even partial failure) is part of testing. The team deliberately planned

A: ACTIVATE INCLUSION AND INNOVATION

for test failures rather than treat every test failure as a catastrophe.

In a free-flight test for one of its vehicles, the Morpheus deviated, tipped over, and crashed shortly after takeoff, resulting in a fiery end to the vehicle and a small grass fire in the fields of the Johnson Space Center. Fortunately, no personnel were injured and only the test hardware was lost. NASA did not treat it as a "mishap" in the worst sense. Following the failure, the team improved the design.

Project Morpheus ultimately successfully completed a series of free-flight tests and demonstrated autonomous hazard detection and precision landing capabilities—all in a relatively low-cost, rapid-development context.

NASA leadership, including then-Administrator Charlie Bolden, explicitly praised Project Morpheus' approach as a model for "learning fast, failing smart" and risk-aware innovation.

This recognition for Project Morpheus pushed NASA forward by serving as a model for a high-risk, high-learning, lean engineering initiative that didn't shy away from failure, but used it to accelerate innovation.

The Lean Forward; Fail Smart Award had a visible winner that helped move NASA away from its "failure is not an option" mentality.

Languages of Appreciation

During my rotation as a front-line leader to JSC Engineering, I started with a listening tour. After meeting with each engineer, it was clear the team was frustrated with a lack of recognition from their management team.

To remedy that, I facilitated a session on *The 5 Languages of Appreciation in the Workplace* by Gary Chapman and Paul White. The book focuses on the core idea that people feel valued in different ways, so others should learn to recognize the primary "language of appreciation" of team members to enhance morale and engagement. The five languages of appreciation are:

- *Words of Affirmation*: Verbal praise
- *Acts of Service*: Helping with tasks
- *Receiving Gifts*: Thoughtful, personalized tokens
- *Quality Time*: Focused interaction
- *Physical Touch*: Appropriate contact in the workplace (e.g., high-fives or "pats on the back")

The session enabled the team members to understand one another's preferences for recognition and initiate peer-to-peer appreciation to enhance their engagement.

It was partly due to this effort that the organization saw dramatic improvement in its employee engagement scores the following year.

#2—Opportunities to Grow

Driver #2 is this: "I am given a real opportunity to improve my skills in my organization."

An employee and his or her supervisor both have a responsibility to engage with each other to discuss opportunities, capitalize on the employee's unique skills, and carve out time for the employee to engage in innovative activities. The employee should come to those conversations with an understanding of his or her strengths and how they can best contribute to success.

These conversations lead to a variety of outcomes, including establishing a percentage of time for engaging in innovative efforts. The groundbreaking company 3M has a long-standing policy of allowing employees to dedicate up to 15 percent of their work time to pursuing innovative, self-chosen projects, fostering creativity and leading to such iconic products as Post-It Notes.

NASA leveraged this idea differently, as they dedicated some funding to new ideas from employees. High-performing employees applied for innovation funds to purchase equipment or reserve lab time to work on their unique ideas.

For others, it might mean pushing boundaries within current job assignments to find ways to improve work efficiency, suggest streamlined work processes, or identify better business practices.

As part of the journey at NASA Johnson Space Center, we understood that it was easy for supervisors and managers to have their "go-to" people for special projects, assignments, and opportunities. That's natural. In fact, psychological research calls it the "like me" bias. According to research, the affinity bias is when people favor, trust, and positively evaluate others who are similar to themselves—in background, beliefs, experiences, personality, or identity—often without realizing it. This is especially powerful in leadership and talent decisions, when leaders may think they are using good judgment or intuition. As a result, awareness is a key first step for leaders to manage this bias.

Organizationally, JSC leadership became intentional about increasing transparency for opportunities. Within months, more promotion opportunities and significant project roles were filled following open competition. In the span of a couple of years, JSC went from competing half of its promotion opportunities to all of them. Additionally, a panel of interviewers, composed of leaders within and outside the organization, was engaged to make the selection decisions and verify the "like me" bias was not prevalent in selection decisions.

Over time, many special projects and assignments were advertised for employee consideration—part of the Transparent Opportunities Program (TOP)—an idea that came from a group of employees and the union through JSC's labor-management partnership.

A: ACTIVATE INCLUSION AND INNOVATION

Building on the success of TOP, JSC deployed the NASA Employee Talent Search tool to improve the effectiveness of its internal placement processes through greater transparency, expanded access, and increased responsiveness. With the tool, JSC employees searched and applied for a variety of career-building opportunities that supported mission and organization needs.

These efforts helped NASA leaders get beyond a select few "go-to" people to broaden their pool of talent for projects, assignments, and promotions. It also fostered a mindset that development was for all team members.

#3—Make Decisions

Driver #3 is based on this question: "How satisfied are you with your involvement in decisions that affect your work?"

JSC encouraged supervisors to "ask questions; don't give answers." A couple of books helped promote this idea. One was John Maxwell's *Good Leaders Ask Great Questions*. A couple of questions he suggests include:

- "What is the greatest lesson you have learned?" This reveals someone else's wisdom, and you can learn from others' experience.
- "What are you learning now?" This enables you to benefit from the other's passion.

Another helpful resource was Dr. Edgar Schein's *Humble Inquiry*—the fine art of drawing someone out, asking questions to which you do not already know the answer, and building a relationship based on curiosity and interest in the other person.

Considered the "godfather of organization culture," Dr. Schein points out that in both of NASA's space shuttle disasters (*Challenger* and *Columbia*), and in the British Petroleum gulf oil spill, a common finding was that lower-ranking employees had information that would have prevented or lessened the consequences of the accidents. Unfortunately, either that information was not passed up to higher levels, or it was ignored or overridden. Leaders must remain open-minded and inquisitive, keeping employees involved in decisions that affect their work.

Following the *Columbia* accident, NASA initiated the Ombuds Program—an informal, independent, confidential, and neutral means of communicating and facilitating the resolution of safety, organizational performance, and mission-related issues without fear of retaliation.

Ombuds listen to an employee's issues, explore options, and weigh the pros and cons of various options for resolution. Individuals use the Ombuds if:

- They do not know what formal resources are available to them.

A: ACTIVATE INCLUSION AND INNOVATION

- They have already been to formal channels and do not feel that the process is fair.
- They feel that the formal channel is too close to the situation to be impartial.
- They want to raise an issue anonymously.

The Ombuds:

- Listen with an open mind.
- Help clarify an issue.
- Work to identify options for resolution and the pros and cons of each.
- Coach employees on how to effectively communicate their concerns.
- Facilitate discussion between individuals.
- Refer to formal resources when appropriate.
- Escalate concerns only with permission of the employee.
- Share general issue trends with management.

The Ombuds Program effectively provided an additional avenue for employees to raise a variety of issues and concerns at NASA.

Due to the success of the Ombuds at NASA, I quickly brought the same program to Space Center Houston. While we had effective formal communication channels with supervisors, managers, security, and human resources, I recognized that trained and certified Ombuds would enhance our ability to hear issues and concerns that may otherwise go unshared. The program was an effective alternative avenue for employees to raise concerns.

#4—Empower

Driver #4 is "Employees have a feeling of personal empowerment with respect to work processes."

When she became center director at JSC, Dr. Ellen Ochoa recognized that if the organization did not change as quickly as the environment, it would fall behind. And if JSC fell behind, NASA would become a symbol of what human space flight used to be, not the organization that leads human space flight into the future.

To move forward, Dr. Ochoa initiated a branding campaign of JSC 2.0 to get the workforce to think differently. The campaign goal was to advance human spaceflight by being lean, agile, and adaptive to change.

As Dr. Ochoa noted, "Only by doing that will we be able to make future exploration missions, leading to a mission to Mars, possible—and possible not just because we solve the many exciting technical and operational challenges, but because we've figured out how to do it in a way that: fits a reasonable budget and makes the best use of every person."

For the JSC 2.0 branding, it is important to consider a new software release. What does a 2.0 software release do? It keeps the best of what is working and makes

A: ACTIVATE INCLUSION AND INNOVATION

improvements to the original design. That was what Dr. Ochoa asked each of us to critically examine—wherever we worked and whatever we did.

Dr. Ochoa set the direction to transform culture, processes, and capabilities to align with NASA's evolving mission portfolio. Her leadership redefined the center's identity from sole operator to integrator and overseer of a broad partner ecosystem. She also strengthened approaches to collaboration with commercial partners, enabling the foundations for today's commercial crew and commercial low-Earth orbit missions. This repositioning helped establish JSC's long-term relevance in a mixed public-private spaceflight environment.

JSC 2.0 introduced tools for innovation, crowdsourcing, and continuous improvement. The initiative addressed structural complexity by improving integration across directorates, clarifying technical authority, and updating governance and decision-making processes to reduce silos, enhance transparency, and enable quicker, more informed decisions.

The initiative accelerated the adoption of digital engineering, collaboration platforms, and improved knowledge management. JSC started laying the groundwork for model-based systems engineering and increased use of data analytics. These steps prepared JSC for more complex, highly integrated space missions.

JSC 2.0 emphasized developing a more adaptable workforce. New competency models, mobility programs, leadership development efforts, and cross-training created greater flexibility across mission areas. These changes helped ensure that JSC had the right skills for both ISS and emerging exploration programs.

Dr. Ochoa positioned Johnson Space Center for long-term leadership by modernizing how the center works—culturally, organizationally, and operationally. Her leadership helped JSC become more collaborative, innovative, and adaptive, enabling success in a complex era.

It should be noted that employees don't have to wait to be empowered. One of NASA's core values is excellence: "To achieve the highest standards in engineering, research, operations, and management in support of mission success." So NASA nurtures an organizational culture in which individuals make full use of their time, talent, and opportunities to pursue excellence in both the ordinary and the extraordinary.

#5—Opportunities to Lead

Driver #5 is "My supervisor or team leader provides me with opportunities to demonstrate my leadership skills."

To build that culture of innovation, employees need not only opportunities to grow but also stretch assignments that reveal leadership skills.

A: ACTIVATE INCLUSION AND INNOVATION

Let's peel this back a bit. Is this about preparing everyone to become a manager? No, leadership is influence. What happens when we change the word: "My supervisor or team leader provides me with opportunities to demonstrate my *influence* skills." Everyone wants his or her voice to be heard in the organization. Everyone has a point of view. That is why NASA consistently asks, "Are leaders engaging everyone on the team?"

NASA's management solicits input from employees on mission safety, program success, and work processes through several means, including focus groups, team recommendations, and participation in anonymous employee surveys.

What are the responsibilities of employees? They must seek opportunities to influence and to offer opinions. When I spoke with NASA leaders, I would often ask, "How many of you, like me, are introverted?" Of course, many of the science and engineering leaders would raise their hands.

As I noted to them, that may mean we need to push ourselves to speak up when we are not quite comfortable doing so—and often before we have the perfectly formulated thought or idea. Pushing ourselves to do that could lead to opportunities to demonstrate leadership skills. At the same time, I encouraged extroverted leaders to make sure they were leaving space for others to speak up and engage in solutions-focused discussions.

Leaders need to provide time and space to obtain the best ideas from everyone. Permit me to reminisce here. When I became Natalie Saiz's deputy HR director, I followed an extroverted leader. I appreciated how Natalie adjusted her own leadership style to accommodate mine. She used to talk through strategies at the end of the day with my predecessor. With me, she found that it was more effective if she told me about the topic and planned a deeper discussion the following day. This gave me the opportunity to deliberate on various options and solutions, leading to more effective brainstorming. It was her straightforward way of providing me with opportunities to lead in a way that I could be successful.

#6—Respect

Driver #6 is "I have a high level of respect for my organization's senior leaders."

Employees are at their most creative and engaged not only when they respect their leaders, but also when they feel respected in return. Having confidence in senior leadership is an important underpinning to this culture of innovation.

A lack of employee confidence in senior leadership quickly becomes apparent. This often triggers a negative cycle: leaders sense the lack of respect, respond in kind, and further perpetuate the downward spiral.

A: ACTIVATE INCLUSION AND INNOVATION

To gain respect from teams, leaders often provided mission updates through regular staff meetings, town halls, and walks through the hallways. You've probably heard the term MBWA (management by wandering around). Popularized by Tom Peters' *In Search of Excellence*, MBWA refers to a style of management that involves managers wandering through the workplace in an unstructured manner to check in with employees. The emphasis is on the word "wandering" as an impromptu act, rather than employees expecting a visit from managers. This method helps facilitate improvements to the morale, sense of organizational purpose, and productivity of the organization.

In contrast, let me offer a new term: MBSAD, or "management by sitting at your desk." Unfortunately, MBSAD has become easier and more common in the workplace, especially in an era of virtual work, as we remain glued to our computers and screens. Too many organizations claim, "It's all about the people." But how many managers and senior leaders are more comfortable sitting at their desks? "My door is open," they think, but they haven't built the kind of trust needed so their team members are comfortable walking through that door.

Senior leaders need to engage with employees to build trust. If employees believe they have creative ideas but lack confidence in their organization's senior leaders, they will likely keep those ideas to themselves.

Did you notice anything missing from the six drivers of innovation? Factors such as salary, workload, and resources, while important, do not differentiate innovative cultures from others, and you can quickly see how these drivers of innovation are truly not rocket science.

How would you describe your culture? Is it a culture of innovation?

Drivers of Innovation Summarized

Leaders provide:

- Recognition;
- Opportunities for growth;
- Ability to make decisions;
- Opportunities to improve work processes;
- Leadership opportunities; and
- Respect.

Followers can:

- Appreciate others;
- Seek opportunities;
- Engage and develop solutions;
- Demonstrate excellence;
- Seek opportunities to influence; and
- Be respectful.

What I appreciated about working at the NASA Johnson Space Center was when our Innovation Index score reached a best-in-class 80 percent, we did not congratulate ourselves. Instead, we recognized that data point simply meant one in five employees could not positively address the questions on the index. We recognized that there was still room for improvement, as we sought to engage the entire team.

Hiring for a Culture of Innovation

For many years, JSC successfully supported the ISS and space shuttle—two large human space flight programs—with minimal development work and a relatively stable or growing budget and workforce. Following the retirement of the space shuttle, JSC's strategy evolved to support ISS and multiple small- and medium-sized programs, which required a workforce that could move beyond sustaining operations and support the design and development phase of the program and project life cycle.

Simultaneously, JSC faced a continuously shrinking budget with constant workforce reductions and significant contractor layoffs. Previously, the hiring and staffing plan allowed each organization to determine its own skill needs and how to best meet them; however, this model no longer worked in the new context.

While center leadership looked to HR to take the lead, I knew that to be effective, this could not be an HR strategy. Leaders needed to set the strategy and drive the culture.

My challenge was to create an innovative workforce strategy that strategically gained input and cooperation from the technical organizations. JSC management needed to own the workforce strategy. My vision was for management to engage in the development of an integrated center workforce plan.

I focused on JSC's long-term interests and leveraged the relationships I had with other leaders to formulate a plan. I assembled six key leaders to develop a framework for JSC's Journey to Mars workforce strategy. I led the group by encouraging members to ask other centers and high-performing organizations for their processes to help us analyze our conventional approaches and design a new process.

From another NASA center, we learned about its long-term workforce planning process that enabled "forward-filling" key skills instead of back-filling losses. We capitalized on the information and developed mission and management assumptions designed for senior leadership discussions that could generate a shared understanding about the skills needed for the future of human space exploration.

Specifically, we developed two contrasting scenarios that showcased the need for a better strategy. The first assumed no hiring and no strategic choices; in other words, we would continue with JSC's same reduction profile for the past five years. The picture clearly painted a significant

A: ACTIVATE INCLUSION AND INNOVATION

negative impact on the skills NASA needed for the future. The second scenario proposed deeper cuts in engineering operations and support functions to enable higher levels of investment in engineering design and development skills.

The core team took these scenarios to a larger forum of representatives from every JSC organization to solicit their input and ideas prior to moving forward. From these discussions, we delivered a framework for workforce strategy discussions to the JSC director and senior staff, which brought about the necessary buy-in.

As a result of this effort, the center director declared the center's top priority: "Develop a workforce strategy for exploration, including a multiyear plan outlining civil servant sizing for the next five to ten years to ensure we have the skills needed for exploration."

To support this new workforce strategy, JSC implemented a hiring model that required 60 percent of hires be recent college graduates in engineering and business disciplines; 20 percent were "forward-fills" based on skills identified in the workforce strategy discussions; and the remaining 20 percent covered unexpected losses in critical skill areas.

Lastly, we developed a process to regularly review our future investment and divestment strategies. Through these efforts, JSC was poised to support NASA's journey to Mars for the following ten years.

From Mission First to People First

For my first twenty-five years at NASA, the culture could best be described as "Mission First, People Always."

In fact, NASA Administrator Charlie Bolden once said, "Those of us who work at NASA know it's a great place to work. We are the world leader in space exploration and cutting-edge science missions and contribute to the economic vitality of our great nation. We challenge our employees to carry out missions that benefit humankind. What job could be better than that?"

To do big things, teamwork has long been a hallmark of NASA's culture. Popular movies have even highlighted this. Both *Apollo 13* (which was mentioned previously) and the more recent movie *Hidden Figures* showcased how NASA's teams of people pulled together—mostly in person—to solve big problems. For more than sixty years, NASA had a long history and culture of in-person teamwork, and its inspiring mission connected people.

Then came the COVID-19 pandemic of 2020. Like most organizations at the time, 95 percent of NASA worked remotely during the pandemic. This created challenges for leaders who had never led virtual teams.

Because NASA people love what they do, many engineers and scientists were having difficulty turning off their computers or stepping away from work. As a result, leaders

A: ACTIVATE INCLUSION AND INNOVATION

were challenged by the "virtual sweatshop" effect this was creating across the agency.

On the one hand, it was fortunate for NASA that most employees had the technology, tools, and capabilities required for virtual work. But leaders needed practical tips on leading people who were working remotely. They needed to better understand the nature of virtual work and to encourage their employees to unplug and take breaks.

It was at this critical time that senior leadership of the agency made an intentional shift from our long-standing strategy of "Mission First, People Always" to a new strategy of "People First, Mission Always." NASA's senior leaders made the health and safety of the NASA workforce paramount. Specifically, they shifted mission milestones and flight schedules to ensure the safety of people.

Human resources stepped in to convene monthly meetings with the 2,000 supervisors across NASA to give them tools on how to conduct performance discussions, how to have difficult conversations, and how to handle stress in the new virtual environment.

NASA being NASA even had astronauts and flight doctors—who deal with the impacts of isolation in space—share their experiences and lessons learned about isolation with supervisors. Interestingly, during these virtual sessions, supervisors began engaging in chats with one another, asking questions about specific scenarios, and providing their own perspectives and solutions.

Over time, our human resources team recognized that topics of discussion were less important than simply providing a venue for an exchange of ideas and information. As a result, HR shifted to providing questions that would lead to peer-to-peer engagement and interaction through chat. These engagements created many cross-center collaborations among supervisors who had otherwise never engaged with one another.

For NASA's 18,000-member workforce, engagement and satisfaction scores dropped slightly from a high of 86.6 to 85.1 in 2021, but NASA remained the best place to work in the U.S. government for the tenth consecutive year. In 2021, leadership scores improved from 82.8 to 84.7 with front-line supervisors climbing from 91.1 to 91.8. As we have known for many years, it was clear that the focus on front-line leaders was key to maintaining high engagement, and it was good to see the data bear that out.

A: ACTIVATE INCLUSION AND INNOVATION

Key NASA Principle: Activate Inclusion and Innovation

Activate cultural transformation by creating an environment that promotes inclusion and fosters innovation. To thrive, it is critical to build safe spaces where diverse perspectives are heard and new ideas can flourish. This is best achieved through transparent and ongoing communication.

At NASA, we asked ourselves some important reflection questions. I encourage you to do the same.

Questions for Reflection:

- How would you describe your organization's culture?
- Do you have clearly articulated expected behaviors?
- What can you learn from the innovation index and how NASA specifically leveraged the six drivers of innovation?
- In what ways do you recognize and celebrate innovative thinking and contributions?
- What are the barriers to inclusion or innovation in your current organizational culture, and how can they be addressed?
- What steps do you need to take to put people first in your organization?

- How do you evaluate the impact of your people-first initiatives on both employee engagement and organizational performance?

As we reflected on these questions, our team moved into action. Consider the following action steps in your own journey.

Action Steps:

- Ensure your organization's values and expected behaviors are clear.
- Evaluate the six drivers for a culture of innovation—and the specific examples NASA used—to determine appropriate actions for your organization.
- Provide training and development programs that promote a culture of inclusion and teach leaders to create an environment where everyone feels valued.
- Establish regular forums or roundtables where employees can share challenges, ideas, and solutions in a safe environment.
- Implement mentorship or peer-support programs to strengthen connections and the sharing of knowledge across teams.
- Encourage risk-taking and problem-solving, ensuring that all members feel empowered to contribute innovative ideas.

A: ACTIVATE INCLUSION AND INNOVATION

- Develop communication channels that ensure everyone is aware of cultural priorities and progress—what you are doing and what you have learned.
- Develop specific recognition programs that highlight both individual and team achievements in innovation and inclusion.
- Regularly review and update policies to ensure they support work-life balance, especially in virtual or flexible work arrangements.
- Set up metrics and feedback loops to monitor the effectiveness of inclusion and innovation strategies, adjusting as needed.
- Encourage leaders to model vulnerability and openness, demonstrating that it is safe to share challenges and learn from setbacks.
- If needed, shift your organization's mindset to "people-first," ensuring that the well-being and engagement of employees are seen as essential for mission success.

Landing

THE SPACE SHUTTLE PRIMARILY landed at the Shuttle Landing Facility at Kennedy Space Center in Florida. If landing conditions in Florida were poor, the shuttle sometimes touched down in California instead. It would then be transported back to Florida atop a Boeing 747 called the Shuttle Carrier Aircraft—which you can see displayed with a replica shuttle mounted on its back at Space Center Houston.

The landing process involved a series of maneuvers, including entering the atmosphere, doing a series of roll reversals to dissipate energy, aligning with the runway, and lowering the landing gear.

The shuttle entered the atmosphere at around 400,000 feet and performed maneuvers to successfully enter the landing approach corridor. The orbiter pitched up to a 40-degree angle of attack to protect itself with its heat shield.

The astronaut commander flying the orbiter then lined up with the center of the runway, and the pilot lowered its landing gear at an elevation of 400 feet.

The grooved concrete runway was designed to maximize braking, increase friction, and provide drainage.

The Shuttle Landing Facility in Brevard County, Florida, was nicknamed the "gator tanning facility" because alligators would bask in the sunlight on the runway.

It was always good to welcome the space shuttle safely home.

Organizationally, "landing" is recognizing that you are on target with the desired organization culture. However, the landing phase was not the end for the space shuttle (until its final flight in 2011). Following a successful landing, each shuttle was fully refurbished for its next scheduled flight. This is a good reminder that culture work is never completed. It is a continuous work in progress.

It Really Can Be Done Anywhere...

Applying NASA's Lessons at Space Center Houston

JUST AS THE SHUTTLE lands safely, it is important to recognize that the concepts NASA used to build culture can be applied to your organization.

In fact, for the last ten years, I have spoken about these concepts at organizations, domestic seminars, and international conferences—from Amsterdam to Barcelona, Chicago to Canada, Denver to Dubai, JSC to Johannesburg, Kuala Lumpur to London, and more.

Over that time, I encouraged audiences that **Building Culture the NASA Way** really can be done anywhere.

Is that really true? Can you take lessons from NASA's workforce of 18,000 employees with 2,000 supervisors to a smaller, non-profit team of 360 (160 full-time and another 200 part-time/seasonal crew members) with 25 people leaders?

Now, over the past three years, I have applied these lessons and approaches, and this has served as a strong proving ground for these concepts.

To recap our framework:

1. **Navigate the Culture**: Understand existing culture, values, and dynamics.
2. **Assess and Adapt**: Measure the culture and focus on the critical elements that drive success.
3. **Strengthen Leadership and Systems**: Engage leadership to model and drive cultural change.
4. **Activate Inclusion and Innovation**: Build a culture that prioritizes inclusivity and innovation, while effectively communicating progress.

Navigate the Culture

Earlier, I wrote about the listening tour, which was critical to my first ninety days. I started by talking with every supervisor, engaging regularly with executives, and meeting with groups of employees. As my predecessor noted in our transition conversations, we needed more emphasis on leadership training and development as well as strategies for employee engagement.

Frankly, that was why I was hired. Anna Haire, Space Center Houston's first and only HR leader, established a strong foundation of HR operations with a family-like culture but recognized that for the next season of Space Center Houston, executive leadership would be needed to provide talent strategies that guide the growth and steward the culture of the organization.

This foresight of my predecessor enabled a successful, planned executive transition.

But it is important to note that my listening did not stop after those first ninety days. For my schedule, I prioritized monthly one-on-one meetings with each member of our Executive Leadership Team and those in Director-level roles. I convened quarterly meetings with those in Manager and Supervisor-level roles as well. These meetings were crucial in understanding the culture, values, and dynamics of Space Center Houston.

I appreciate the perspective of Spanish-American philosopher, poet, novelist, and cultural critic George Santayana, who wrote, "Those who cannot remember the past are condemned to repeat it."

Therefore, it was important for me to also understand the history of the organization, which was borne from an idea of NASA's Johnson Space Center (JSC) leaders, who saw the need to preserve and present the story of human spaceflight to the public. In the late-1980s, they found they could not sustain the numbers of guests coming on-site to NASA.

As a solution, they initiated an official visitor center as a nonprofit—the Manned Space Flight Education Foundation, Incorporated (MSFEFI). From the outset, no federal funds were used to build or operate the center. To pay for construction of the facility that would become Space Center Houston, the Foundation sold nearly $70 million in tax-exempt bonds in 1991, and Space Center Houston opened to the public in October 1992.

The business model was designed so modest admission fees and educational program revenues would fund operations and service the bond debt. Therefore, the organization faced significant pressure to generate steady admission and program revenue immediately upon opening, which was a common model for nonprofit museums and visitor centers at that time.

Unfortunately, attendance projections did not materialize in the early years, and the finance team had to await cash receipts from admissions to pay the bills and cover weekly payroll. Ultimately, the bonds were restructured, and Space Center Houston survived for many years with a scarcity mindset. Every dollar was scrutinized and carefully stewarded.

Then, William T. Harris joined as President & CEO in 2016, bringing decades of nonprofit leadership experience, especially in development, fundraising, marketing, and strategic planning. He was hired to strengthen Space Center Houston's financial footing, expand its reach, and build a sustainable model for long-term growth.

Under Harris's leadership, annual attendance increased significantly, doubling during his tenure from about 600,000 guests per year to more than 1.25 million guests. Additionally, Harris diversified revenue streams for the organization, creating new corporate sponsorship and revenue-earning education programs along with grants, royalties, and investment income.

As Houston's number one attraction for international visitors, Space Center Houston serves as a destination, generating nearly $120 million in annual economic impact for the Greater Houston area.

In 2023, I entered an organization with strong attendance growth and diversified revenues. With net revenues, we also had a quasi-endowment to support future expansion plans. By 2025, we made the final bond payment and were declared "debt free."

During my first two years, we increased the staff size by ten percent per year—from 160 full-time crew members to 200 by 2025. Then, in 2025, we saw a slight decrease in guest attendance—mainly due to industry-wide decline in both domestic and international travel. Therefore, we adjusted HR strategies and budgets to align with these realities—slightly reducing investments in training and leveling our staffing trajectory.

This was an important learning from the organization's history—to modulate our strategies and plans, aligned with realities of guest attendance flows and projections.

Assess and Adapt

At NASA, we encouraged leaders at all levels to identify two or three areas for improvement from their employee engagement survey results and tie improvement initiatives to the survey feedback. We wanted them to make sure employees knew their survey results and where they would target improvements—engaging employees in planning those improvements, where practical.

As previously noted, when I joined Space Center Houston in 2023, the most recent employee engagement survey was conducted in 2019. Following the listening tour of my first ninety days, I developed the following priorities:

Improve onboarding to a more systematic process.

- Increase flexibilities for paid time off.
- Offer incentives for improved physical health and education.
- Provide resources for mental health & stress management.

We called for volunteers to participate in our Crew Engagement Team, who would be responsible for investigating these new policies and perquisites—or "perks." However, the team could not simply assemble charts and information, they needed to develop business cases for change to leadership. This secured their buy-in and provided unique leadership development opportunities.

The team ultimately produced a new paid time off policy, reimbursements for physical health purchases (beyond the original idea of gym membership reimbursements), and a first-ever episodic work-from-home policy for non-exempt staff. In addition, the volunteers learned how to develop and present business cases to leadership along the way.

Nevertheless, we still needed a way to measure employee engagement across the organization. We started with Gallup's Q12—a simple, proven framework that was detailed previously—and enhanced our own survey with items from the federal government's employee engagement survey covering effective leadership, teamwork, commitment to excellence, inclusion, and overall satisfaction and engagement.

We administered our first survey in 2023 and received a forty-two percent response rate. The survey revealed that crew members understood what was expected of them, and they felt a sense of importance tied to the organization's mission. Supervisors showed good respect and care for employees, and two-thirds of the respondents recommended Space Center Houston as a place to work.

At the same time, the survey also revealed that work was needed around recognition and sharing of opinions by employees. In early 2024, we convened a new team of volunteers to take on these "critical few" issues. They evaluated our recognition program and practices as well as our performance planning and appraisal system.

We initiated a "Giving & Receiving Feedback" course to ensure opinions could be shared and heard better. For recognition, we held our first-ever Crew Awards and Recognition Event (CARE) in August 2024, celebrating the many achievements and exceptional service of Space Center Houston's Crew Members. This event coincided with the celebration of making our final bond payment—a 30-year journey to become "debt free" for the bonds that built our original visitor center facilities.

We administered our second employee engagement survey in 2024, which pointed to a few primary themes for improvement:

- *Awards and recognition:* Improve recognition for good work across Space Center Houston.
- *Performance and development:* According to the survey, only 60 percent of crew members agreed that they received constructive suggestions to improve performance. Our performance review system—like all appraisal systems that I have ever experienced—had mixed reviews. In fact, only one-third of the reviews were complete; another third was left in some stage of the cycle—between self-assessment and required signatures; and another third were never even started.

Just as before, we assembled Crew Engagement teams to address those themes. In 2024, more than 100 crew members participated in a course on "Giving and Receiving Feedback." Then, we completed our first-ever upward feedback initiative for each people leader, using an executive coach to help leaders focus on the right feedback and customize a plan for improvement.

As a result of these efforts, we saw improved scores from 2024 to 2025 on these items: nine percent increase for "At work, my opinions seem to count" and six percent increase for "My supervisor provides me with constructive suggestions to improve my performance."

The performance review process team tied performance reviews to annual merit pay increases for the first time. The team developed a new plan for performance reviews that provided a range of merit increases based on performance, and they simplified the use of competencies in the system.

Since our lowest-scoring item from the survey was: "Excellent work is not similarly recognized for all crew members," our team worked to deliver the first-ever Crew Awards and Recognition Event, which recognized several crew members in the areas of leadership, service, and achievement, along with some creative write-in categories. The event was a success with approximately half of the organization being recognized, either individually or as part of a team.

In another encouraging development, crew members felt their colleagues were highly cooperative—this was the most-improved item from 2023 to 2024. Our efforts to enhance cross-departmental collaboration were working! Additionally, crew members felt a sense of importance tied to the mission and purpose of Space Center Houston. Three-quarters reported they would recommend Space

Center Houston as a good place to work (an increase of nearly 10 percent from the initial survey).

In the open-ended responses on the survey, crew members requested improved communication, especially between leadership and front-of-house roles. As a result, we prioritized hiring an Internal Communications Manager, who started in 2025. Following her own listening tour, she immediately made improvements in communication strategies, methods, and approaches that reached crew members in new ways, providing timely information about day-to-day operations, future strategies, and leadership priorities. We are already seeing significant benefits from this important organization investment.

In 2025, we partnered with an external organization to conduct our engagement survey. Our response rate slightly dipped to 38 percent, but the results were encouraging. Our focus on improving internal communications showed measurable improvement, as crew members reported feeling well-informed about important decisions at Space Center Houston. They further reported that Space Center Houston is headed in the right direction.

The top three words used to describe the organization's culture were: "inclusive," "diverse," and "welcoming." That was validating for the focus on our organization values of being people-driven champions of curiosity.

The external entity reported that Space Center Houston was best-in-class for employee pay and benefits.

We are committed to further studying and analyzing the results to become an even better place to work.

Strengthen Leadership and Systems

For more than twenty years, nearly two-thirds of the Federal Government's employee engagement scores have been driven by employees' perspective of their leaders. Based on this, organizations must commit to invest in leadership development. It starts with the leaders.

At Space Center Houston, like NASA, we leveraged the Center for Creative Leadership's 70/20/10 model, which says:

- 70% of an individual's development is based on job experiences (Content);
- 20% of development is gained through relationships with other people, like mentors and coaches (Contacts); and
- 10% of development comes through leadership training courses (Concepts).

We took specific steps to execute the strategy, focusing on developing crew members through:

Content

We developed Space Center Houston's first-ever career development guide, revealing career paths and options available to crew members and showcasing the types of training and development they should pursue. We also created job rotations for key roles, including a first-ever Project Manager for the CEO.

Contacts

I was able to bring a virtual coaching program that NASA used to all of Space Center Houston's people leaders. That was a quick win during my first year. Leaders engaged with coaches in customized development conversations nearly twice per month and demonstrated improvement in their leadership skills.

At the same time, we launched a cross-department mentoring program for leaders, seeking to enhance leadership relationships across organization boundaries. My predecessor recommended pairings of leaders to enhance collaboration and relationships. Throughout the program, we provided monthly guidance and support to more than twenty pairs of managers and leaders.

Finally, we provided upward feedback for every people leader, so they could understand perspectives of crew members under their care. We engaged an external coach, who interpreted data for each leader and helped them build individual development plans. Our external coach noted that the leaders were receptive to the feedback, and the crew members appreciated the opportunity—a first for most of them—to provide anonymous feedback to their leaders. The feedback was effective because it was not provided for performance appraisal—but solely intended for leadership development and improvement.

Based on our initial experience, we recognized that many leaders had a small number of direct reports (we did not provide reports to anyone with fewer than three respondents). So, when we repeated the feedback opportunity in 2025, we incorporated peer perspectives, so every leader invited at least eight raters. Additionally, we added a few open-ended questions, including: "What do you appreciate most about this leader?" and "What is one area of growth or development that you would recommend for this leader?"

The survey changes were welcomed by our people leaders, who resonated with the different perspectives they received. One theme emerged from the feedback that people shared excitement about Space Center Houston's growth but felt apprehension about the scheduled timeline and milestones. It was helpful to see organization themes not only from our annual crew engagement survey but from other instruments like this leader feedback tool.

Concepts

For leadership training, we initiated a one-day course on the fundamentals of leadership for aspiring leaders and another three-day course for people leaders focused on improving leadership effectiveness. Leaders needed to start with themselves, understand their own leadership strengths and capacities, then learn how to best lead their teams and organizations. The new course provided effective frameworks for leaders to enhance their own capabilities and capacities.

In 2025, several members from our Board of Directors recommended a leadership development program with Verus Global. Their Pathways to Leadership Transformations Program—based on the book *Do Big Things: The Simple Steps Teams Can Take to Mobilize Hearts and Minds, and Make an Epic Impact* by Craig Ross, Angela Paccione, and Victoria Roberts—is a developmental process that strengthens and sustains a team's deep alignment to its imperatives.

At Space Center Houston, our business imperative is to "plan boldly, act wisely, and grow sustainably.

As one crew, we execute our two-year operational plan with clarity, collaboration, and strategic resourcefulness, building the capacity, trust, and community support that fuel sustainable growth and achievement of our capital campaign goals."

Our human imperative is to "engage many, decide clearly, and commit fully. We welcome diverse perspectives, challenge ideas with respect, and once the decision is made, we move together with trust and accountability."

The Program uses a three-day launch to develop a common language for decision-making and peer-to-peer accountability. The launch is followed by ten weeks of Perpetual Alignment, Collaboration, and Trust (P.A.C.T.)

meetings for groups of four or five cross-functional leaders. Then, there is a two-day mastery session, followed by eight more weeks of P.A.C.T. team meetings.

Throughout 2025, we took three different cohorts of leaders through the program, covering nearly seventy crew members. We went a step further, shuffling P.A.C.T. teams and continuing dialogue about the tools and techniques provided by Verus Global to enhance our organization culture. The results were striking, as we noted measurable improvement in organizational alignment and outcomes. We plan to continue engaging with Verus Global for new cohorts of leaders every year, as we continue to blend and mix P.A.C.T. teams to enhance relationships and cross-departmental collaboration.

In addition to the Pathways to Leadership Transformation Program, we turned to our 2025 external engagement survey responses. They identified a couple of improvements needed from front-line leaders. First, crew members wanted their leaders to show more support for their concerns. Second, they wanted help with their career growth and development. To that end, we launched two brand-new leadership cohorts—one for supervisors and another for team leads.

The Vanguard Leadership Academy is Space Center Houston's flagship development experience for front-line leaders. The program strengthens leadership effectiveness through applied practice, systems thinking, and culture-driven behaviors—emphasizing real-world application and measurable organizational impact aligned to mission and values. The program is designed to enhance:

- *Emotional intelligence* and leadership presence: Builds self-awareness, empathy, composure, and trust-building skills.
- *Resilience and adaptive leadership:* Develops adaptability and steadiness under pressure.
- *Change leadership and organizational navigation:* Equips leaders to implement and sustain change.
- *Inclusive leadership and culture building:* Fosters belonging and engagement through inclusive practice.
- *Accountability, ownership, and organizational impact:* Establishes accountability systems and measurable outcomes.

Cohort participants take part in monthly leadership missions, which are scenario-based applications that move leadership development from theory to practice. We will celebrate our first cohort graduation later this year.

In the Fall of 2025, our Executive Leadership Team started to more closely evaluate our pool of potential successors. We engaged in a Succession Development evaluation of all Directors using the MentiMeter tool to capture anonymous feedback, which was intended to foster a development mindset for everyone.

We captured perspectives of our Executive Leadership Team about the next level of leaders, so we could purposefully grow and develop them through meaningful discussions that focused on the right next assignments and opportunities for their individual growth and development.

Through these efforts to strengthen leadership and systems, we are enhancing leadership capacities for today as we prepare leaders of tomorrow.

Activate Inclusion and Innovation

Shortly after arriving at Space Center Houston, I recognized that the culture strategy pursued by the Johnson Space Center, which focused on inclusion and innovation, would work well in this new context too. I advised our CEO, William Harris, that we embed the inclusion function in the Human Resources Department and retitle my position as Chief Human Resources and Inclusion Officer (CHRIO). Plus, he could then refer to me as the organization's "cheerio."

William agreed to these changes and authorized me to hire a Manager of Crew Engagement and Inclusion in late-2025, just as the political rhetoric was heating up around diversity, equity, and inclusion. We agreed that our core values supported this next step:

- *People-Driven:* Believes in the inclusive, collaborative power of people.

- *Champions of Curiosity:* Nurtures inquisitive minds, as curiosity leads to innovation, inspiration, and achievement.
- *Space Enthusiasts:* Shares excitement and an unyielding pursuit of excellence to instill a passion for space in others.

From our core values, you can see how easy it was to pursue a culture strategy of inclusion and innovation. My next step was to embed the culture strategy in many of our HR deliverables—from on-boarding to training to performance management.

As we explored potential expected behaviors that could drive our culture, our Chief Marketing and Communications Officer noted that we should have clear alignment between our external branding and our workforce culture. Since our values were developed as part of a re-branding effort in 2022, it was easy to leverage that work to drive the culture forward.

We incorporated our core values into performance evaluations for all crew members and leaders. We also assessed core values in upward feedback to leaders. Accountability for living the values was evident wherever you went.

To steward the culture, we developed a five-phase organizational development roadmap designed to cultivate a resilient, inclusive, and future-ready leadership culture at Space Center Houston. Through multi-track leadership cohorts, quarterly development sessions, strengths-based programs, personalized coaching, team-building, and Socratic-style seminars, the strategy builds everyday leadership capacity and strengthens long-term talent pipelines.

The plan progresses in the following five phases:

1. *Foundation and launch* establish core programs, including our first-ever inclusive leadership cohort and monthly inclusive leadership concepts for peer-to-peer discussions.
2. *Integration* expands and operationalizes multiple leadership streams.
3. *Scaling* deepens impact through peer coaching and advanced team applications.
4. *Embedding* formalizes a leadership academy and publishes impact reporting.
5. *Sustainability and legacy* institutionalize inclusive leadership practices, succession health tracking, and immersive learning innovations, incorporating Artificial Intelligence (AI) and virtual reality (VR).

This plan will strategically sustain an inclusive culture that will drive innovation for the future of Space Center Houston.

In Closing

These are a few of the practical ways that we leveraged some of NASA's best practices on culture measurement and employee engagement in a much different, smaller organization context at Space Center Houston.

As I learned through my NASA experience, culture is created by what leaders do when it is hard, not what they say when it is easy.

I assure you…you can do this.

Keep shooting for the stars!

Afterword

WILLIAM HARRIS HAS A long track record of people-first leadership, including his past twenty-five years as a non-profit executive. He and his team at Space Center Houston brilliantly navigated the global pandemic, as each crew member agreed to take a 10 percent cut in pay to avoid any layoffs from the organization. The team weathered the storm, and they were even able to pay back those pay cuts. When I was looking to join an organization after NASA, that commitment to people said a lot, as it went beyond the words spoken to actions taken.

In late 2022, William and the Space Center Houston team were planning to grow, and he knew he needed an experienced executive who could build leaders and ensure a strong organization culture. Fortunately, I was looking for a new post-NASA challenge, and this was a great fit.

Over the last three years, William and I have partnered on the strategies and tactics outlined in this book, as we have increased the staff by 25 percent while building a more cohesive and collaborative team.

For the last words, I will turn it over to William.

Afterword by William T. Harris

Humanity has always looked to the stars for insight, guidance, and inspiration. Now we can travel into the heavens. Every mission—whether it was the first tentative steps beyond Earth's atmosphere or the complex voyages that followed—began with a team willing to imagine something larger than themselves. The same spirit underlies the work in *Building Culture the NASA Way*. The practices explored are not just strategies for today's challenges; they are the scaffolding for the kinds of teams capable of tackling the equivalent of deepspace missions.

Space exploration underscores how monumental achievements are never the result of a single breakthrough. They emerge from thousands of coordinated decisions, from people aligned around a shared vision, purpose, and mission, from systems built to withstand uncertainty, and from a culture that treats learning as propulsion. As we look ahead, the teams that will shape the future—whether in science, business, public service, or creative fields—will need to operate with that same blend of rigor, curiosity, and resilience.

The next frontier will not announce itself with a countdown. It will arrive in the form of problems that seem complex, interconnected, or unprecedented to solve with conventional approaches. But just as every successful mission has shown, the impossible becomes possible when a team is prepared, aligned, and willing to push beyond the

AFTERWORD

familiar. The ideas and practical advice in *Building Culture the NASA Way* serve as a launchpad for that kind of work: a reminder that extraordinary outcomes are built by ordinary people who commit to extraordinary collaboration.

We all are standing on the edge of the launchpad. The question is not whether the next great challenge will come; it's how ready we will be when it does. And if we build our teams with intention, humility, and a shared sense of purpose, then the future waiting beyond the horizon is one we can reach together.

Inspiration for HR Professionals

My Journey to a Career in Human Resources (HR)

I WENT TO TEXAS A&M University, where I studied political science with a particular emphasis in public administration. From an early age, I wanted to work in government service, and Texas A&M provided opportunities through their Cooperative Education Program to explore different options.

After my freshman year, I worked for the City of Corpus Christi in their accounting department—largely because that was my older brother's college major. While I appreciated the experience and the people there, I knew that accounting was not the right career fit for me. That experience convinced me to encourage students to complete many different internships while in college—they need to understand what they like as well as what they don't like to make informed career choices.

During my sophomore year, I interviewed with the Department of Health & Human Services' assistant secretary for personnel administration in Washington, D.C. While they were impressed with my interview, they typically hired graduate students, so they asked if I would be willing to work in their Regional Personnel Office in Dallas, Texas. That spring, I started my federal service career as a personnel specialist (GS-3) with the Department of Health & Human Services (HHS).

After my first work tour in Dallas, I was offered a position in Washington, D.C. It was a great experience, as I had long dreamed of working in the nation's capital. However, it was also clear to me that I did not enjoy the policy HR work as much as the operational work I performed in the regional office.

The experience I gained through those initial co-op tours demonstrated that I needed an advanced degree. I explored several options but decided that moving into Texas A&M's business school and pursuing a master of science degree in human resources management (MS/HRM) was the right path. Our MS/HRM program chair was Patrick M. Wright, who has published several books including *The Chief HR Officer: Defining the New Role of Human Resource Leaders* and *Building Profit through Building People*.

In graduate school, I learned about the role of HR generalist (or internal management consulting). Shortly after learning of that role, I initiated a study of federal government HR organizations in Texas to determine how they were structured. I reached out to several agencies, including NASA.

Ultimately, NASA offered me an opportunity as a graduate co-op. (As a side note, I later learned that on my letter inviting NASA to participate in my study of federal

HR offices in Texas, the HR director wrote, "What a clever job search approach!")

I came to NASA for a summer semester. Following a fall semester back at Texas A&M, I returned in the spring and remained at the NASA Johnson Space Center.

Over the next ten years, I served as an HR representative for several organizations at JSC, including the International Space Station (ISS) program and the Engineering Directorate. For the next three years, I served as a front-line supervisor in HR management and development, responsible for a $5 million annual training budget. In these roles, I led twenty professionals who provided advice on HR policies and programs, employee relations, performance management, classification, staffing, hiring, individual training, and organization development services.

Shortly thereafter, I completed a one-year leadership development program, serving in an assignment at NASA Headquarters followed by a five-month tour at the World Bank's International Finance Corporation (IFC). With the IFC, I gained a different perspective of HR and developed a risk-management methodology to support HR's decentralization of authorities to field offices around the world.

Shortly after my return, I was named deputy director of human resources at JSC. Within three years, it was unclear if I would enter the executive ranks, as I always dreamed, so I started thinking about other career paths and opportunities. Then, I read Patrick Wright's *The Chief HR Officer* and learned that 70 percent of private sector HR leaders spent some time in their career outside the HR function.

My entire career had been in HR, so I recognized the need for different experiences to be better prepared for future HR leadership roles. At the same time, NASA was discussing the criticality of the front-line leader's role in both organizational culture and employee engagement. I sought to gain front-line leader perspective in NASA's technical organization and landed an assignment as a front-line leader in engineering at JSC.

At that time, I also read Alan Collins' *Start Your Own Awesome HR Blog*, in which he makes the case that HR leaders should have their own blogs. So, I started a blog and created my own personal brand. "Out of This World Leadership" describes my unique set of passions.

At the onset of my blog, I had enjoyed the privilege of a twenty-year association with NASA's Johnson Space Center—home to the astronauts, the Mission Control Center, and leaders in human space flight. I strive to "Serve Leaders who Shoot for the Stars" with a philosophy, style, and practice of servant leadership.

A few years later at work, I landed my dream job—serving as the fifth HR director for the Johnson Space Center, becoming a member of the federal government's Senior Executive Service (SES). As the keystone of the

Civil Service Reform Act of 1978, the SES was established to "ensure that the executive management of the Government of the United States is responsive to the needs, policies, and goals of the Nation and otherwise is of the highest quality."

Just three years later, NASA shifted the way it managed human resources and other support functions across the agency. Instead of its sixty-year decentralized approach where HR directors reported to their field center directors, the function was centralized and managed as a corporate entity to save resources that could be used for direct mission investments.

I was named the first-ever executive responsible for HR services across NASA, leading the ten field center SES HR directors. It was a different experience supervising a team of executives while managing 80 percent of NASA's $80 million HR budget and 550-member workforce. In 2020, I was promoted to deputy chief human capital officer at NASA, where I served until taking early retirement from NASA in 2023—after completing thirty years of federal service.

During my NASA career, I was honored with the JSC Director's Commendation Award, JSC Director's Innovation Award, NASA Space Flight Awareness Award, and two Outstanding Leadership Medals. I also enjoyed the opportunity to provide keynote speeches to hundreds of NASA astronauts, engineers, rocket scientists, and business professionals about leadership.

I was pleased to join Space Center Houston as its first HR executive in February 2023. Ultimately, I earned the position of chief human resources and inclusion officer (or CHRIO, pronounced "cheerio"), where I continue to serve the crew of Space Center Houston as we engage more than one million guests each year, sharing the stories about the past, present, and future of human space exploration.

Human Resources as a Strategic Partner

When I was in graduate school, I developed a final presentation to fulfill my master's degree requirements on "Achieving Strategic Partnership as a Human Resources Representative: How I can use my MS/HRM Degree at NASA Johnson Space Center." Literature at the time focused on the strategic partnership between the head of HR and the CEO. For my presentation, I sought to show that strategic partnerships could be attained at multiple levels between HR consultants and their assigned management officials. That research and perspective served me well, as I started my HR career at JSC.

Ten years later, I was involved in a study of HR effectiveness at NASA. We identified these indicators of business partnership between HR and the organization:

- The human resources leader reports directly to the top leader of the organization.

- HR's advice and input impact decisions and direction of the organization.
- The top leader actively involves the HR leader in discussions of business and mission priorities—not just traditional HR or employee issues.
- HR is a key player in establishing staffing levels, organization design, and strategic planning.
- Senior managers and key customers recognize the value of results delivered through HR systems, programs, and policies.
- HR specialists are sought out for advice and consultation at all levels of the organization.
- HR specialists are key participants in organization teams and activities beyond traditional HR roles.
- Senior managers—including program and project managers—involve HR in their strategic and implementation activities, including program start-ups and transitions.

The bottom line is that the top HR leader is a key player on the senior management team.

Since joining NASA, I could honestly say that the JSC HR team fulfilled those success criteria, largely because its mission was to ensure a capable and committed workforce when and where needed.

HR team members were expected to serve as examples and role models of the NASA core values (safety, integrity, excellence, teamwork) and JSC expected behaviors.

JSC HR's guiding principles included:

- *Customer Service*: Partner with customers—including managers and employees—to provide timely HR solutions that attract, develop, and retain an adaptable, engaged, and diverse workforce.
- *Initiative*: Apply HR expertise to increase efficiency, improve effectiveness, and reduce costs.
- *Inclusion*: Work together as a team, promoting work-life fit and having fun.

Steps to Success for HR Professionals

Over my initial years in HR—based on my own experiences, observations of others, and discussions with HR professionals across NASA, we developed these steps to success for HR professionals. The beauty of this model is that it could be applied both to career stage—from starting out as an entry-level HR professional to reaching the pinnacle as an HR executive—and to each potential partnership.

The first step is for HR leaders to get to know the leaders of the organization they support. Meet with them often on their turf and attend their business and staff meetings, so you can speak the language of the business.

Respond to the organization's senior leaders and build a reputation for delivering results. Strategically get time with them and make good use of their time. Keep their confidence and determine how to make things easier for them. Do as much on their behalf as you can.

Find ways to influence senior leaders and add value to key forums by participating, volunteering, and providing suggestions and asking questions for clarity and understanding. Be proactive, take initiative, and produce results that help the mission.

Ensure you provide quality products and offer options to meet an end state—don't just solve immediate issues or provide near-term fixes. Maintain a business perspective and customer focus on all that you do.

In building the HR team, raise the professionalism of the organization by hiring professionals with HR degrees, certifications, or equivalent experience. Hire for analytical skills and consulting abilities first, HR knowledge second. Teach and refresh the team on HR fundamentals.

Encourage partnerships with all levels of the organization. HR specialists must learn everything they can about organizations and the people they support. They need foundational HR knowledge and knowledge of the organization's policies, and they must balance representation of both managers and employees.

HR professionals need to get to know the people and the business—and deliver results for both. As I progressed in my own HR career, I recognized the "Steps to Success for HR Professionals" applied both to individuals and new consulting assignments. In fact, this model would have helped ease some frustrations early in my consulting career.

When I was first assigned as management consultant to the International Space Station Program, I quickly identified opportunities for organization improvement and presented a strategic plan to the program manager. Unfortunately, I took the leap to the top of the staircase without establishing my own credibility in the initial steps.

I had to step back, follow the program manager's lead, be responsive, provide quality products and services, and become familiar with the business. Within a few short years, the program manager would tell me, "Listen. I don't want you to tell me what you think I want to hear. I need to know your opinion of what we should do." A business partnership was achieved! But that took many months rather than the many days I originally expected as a young, eager HR consultant.

The Foundation—Core Values

NASA's HR professionals abided by these core values:

- *Integrity*: We were committed to keeping promises, being honest with people, and playing by the rules. We believed it was important to "do the right thing" as we do our jobs.
- *Excellence*: Our reputation for excellence was important to us. We earned our reputation for

excellence through the quality of our work, which reflected our competence, creativity, and commitment to our customers.
- *Bias for Action*: We approached our work with enthusiasm and energy. We were resourceful, enterprising, and showed a bias for action. We built a reputation for taking the initiative, developing alternative solutions, and getting things done. If it could be done, we found a way.
- *Dedication to Customer Service*: We were dedicated to our work and our people, understanding that customer satisfaction was vital to our success. When meeting customers' challenges, our team balanced the needs of JSC and the customer. We counted on each other to get the job done.
- *Teamwork*: We made a commitment to each other. We were one team on the same side. We shared common goals, worked together, supported each other, and celebrated each other's accomplishments. There are no limits to the power of teamwork.

Steps to Success for HR Professionals

The First Step

Responsiveness

To establish credibility, HR professionals need to understand the needs of the customer and show responsiveness, responding to questions and requests quickly.

Be flexible, adapting to the needs of customers. When a question is asked, find the answer. In fact—and this is important advice—it is okay to say, "I don't know" and then research the answer and follow up. That is much better than shooting from the hip on an answer.

Be open-minded and ready to react to suggestions, influences, appeals, or efforts. Be positive about change—be ready and willing to try new ideas.

Timeliness

Build a reputation for timely work—exceed customers' expectations. Meet deadlines and demonstrate reliability.

Don't give excuses—get help from other team members when needed.

Establish your priorities and manage your time. At NASA, I always pointed out to leaders, HR professionals, and other team members alike: "NASA will take as much as you're willing to give." I believe that's true of most organizations.

Early in my NASA career, one trainer said that NASA employees are effective because they take more work on, which he called "more on" behavior.

Are you exhibiting "more on" behavior? What do you need to do to establish appropriate boundaries? That's a key first step to your success as a HR professional.

The Second Step

Quality Products and Services

Build a reputation for high-quality work by exceeding customers' expectations. This means being error-free with the basics.

Earn the trust of your customer and do the right thing.

Communications

Seek advice and ask questions of others to develop your own style and approach.

Share the issues you are working on and lessons learned with the team. Bring new ideas and solutions forward to the team.

Be succinct and clear in your writing, e-mails, discussions, and presentations—remember that less is often better.

Listen carefully and contribute to a climate of trust and open, honest communication.

Participate by clearly and persuasively expressing your ideas and information.

The Third Step

Customer Familiarity

Know your customers' business, goals, strengths, and weaknesses.

Know your customers' training and development needs, and bring ideas forward to address those needs.

Make saying "no" an exception. Instead, offer options. Where possible, find a way to get to "yes."

Be approachable and keep your customers informed.

Collaborate and seek "win/win" solutions.

Team Player

Contribute ideas and solutions.

Recognize and respect differences in others. Listen and share information. Value the ideas and contributions of others.

Ask questions and seek clarification. Participate fully and keep commitments.

Be flexible and respect the partnership created by a team.

Have fun and care about the team and the outcomes.

The Fourth Step: Creativity and Proactive Approach

Apply your individual talents and creativity. Be creative and innovative—bring new ideas and solutions forward to the team.

Stay up-to-date with the latest trends and developments in leadership and management—know your organization's business.

Take risks. Provide recommendations that require leaders to take a leap of faith.

Explore a wide range of options. Bring new ideas and solutions forward to your customers before you're even asked.

Recognize and act on issues before they become problems, and become a partner with the organization's management team.

A Few Thoughts on HR Service Delivery

For many years in the JSC HR office, we enjoyed a unique consulting model. We had HR representatives who were management consultants for the organization. We also had HR development representatives—organization development experts who consulted with leadership on how to improve the overall work environment to enhance employee engagement.

When we decided to have those two consulting perspectives work together as teams with the organizations, that was the most powerful model.

Unfortunately, cost and resource pressures ultimately forced us to combine those two important roles into a single HR business partner (HRBP). Our HRBPs brought both HR management and organization development capabilities and perspectives to their consulting engagements.

A key to our organization's success was staying up with the latest HR trends. We followed the research and writings of Dave Ulrich and used his model from the book *Human Resource Champions* to highlight the different roles of our HR team: strategic partner, change agent, employee champion, and administrative expert.

As an HR executive, I seized opportunities to speak at a number of conferences, including those held by the Human Capital Institute; Evanta's Chief HR Officers' Leadership Summit; and global HR summits in Amsterdam, Barcelona, Dubai, Johannesburg, Kuala Lumpur, London, and Vancouver. Through these experiences, I learned new ideas and approaches used by HR executives and leaders from around the world.

This continual focus on learning from best-in-class organizations helped us maintain effective human resources services delivery for NASA customers.

INSPIRATION FOR HR PROFESSIONALS

As HR professionals, we must keep learning and growing. Our context continues to change—from the effects of the global pandemic to the advent of artificial intelligence and whatever comes next—and we will continue to face new challenges. Together, let's keep people at the forefront and Build Culture the NASA Way.

Key NASA Principles:

- To be a business partner, you have to know the business.
- Note the stair steps to success for HR professionals.
- Keep learning state-of-the-art HR practices.

Questions for Reflection:

- What are your observations and experiences as an HR professional? What can you learn from them?
- What can you learn from the experiences of NASA as shared here?
- How do you effectively integrate HR management and organization development in your current role?
- How do you ensure that you truly understand the business needs of the organization you support?
- In what ways have you collaborated with other professionals to drive organizational change?
- How do you measure the impact of your HR initiatives on organizational success?

- Which HR trends or best practices have recently influenced your approach to HR service delivery?
- What strategies do you use to keep your HR knowledge and skills up-to-date?

About the Author

BRADY PYLE CURRENTLY SERVES as Chief Human Resources & Inclusion Officer (CHRIO) at Space Center Houston—a leading non-profit science and space exploration learning center that serves as Official Visitor Center for NASA's Johnson Space Center, hosting more than one million guests each year.

During Brady's 30-year career at NASA, he observed, led, and coached rocket scientists, engineers, and astronauts, twice earning the NASA Outstanding Leadership Medal. From 2018 to 2023, he served as NASA's first-ever leader of HR field executives, driving the transition to a unified OneHR model. This transformation cut HR costs by 25% and introduced a new HR Business Partner framework—all while helping NASA maintain its standing as the Best Place to Work in the Federal Government for eleven consecutive years.

Brady created OutOfThisWorldLeadership.com, a leadership blog featuring over 350 book summaries, widely recognized as a top resource in its field.

In 2024, Brady received HRO Today's Learning & Development Executive of the Year for Lifetime Achievement. In 2025, his team was named one of the

Top 50 Human Resources Teams in the 2025 OnCon Icon Awards.

In 2025, he published his first book *Out of This World Leadership: Living the Fruit of the Spirit to Lead Well*. Former Astronaut and Retired Aerospace Executive Mike Bloomfield wrote, "Actionable and bursting with compelling stories and insights, Brady humbly and effectively explores effective servant leadership. A game changer to help all leaders succeed at home, at work, and with themselves. Read his book and become an out of this world leader!"

Brady and his wife, Jennifer, live in Houston, Texas and have three adult children.

Need a Speaker, Coach, or Consultant?

Speaker

With over three decades of experience in leadership, coaching, and working alongside rocket scientists, astronauts, and non-profit executives, I bring a wealth of knowledge to my workshops, seminars, and keynote speeches.

I have delivered keynote addresses at numerous national and international conferences and led interactive workshops for audiences ranging from fifteen to five hundred participants.

Coach

As an executive coach, my goal is to understand your perspectives—how you perceive yourself, your team, and your organization. I am doubly certified by the John Maxwell Team and the Workplace Coach Institute (as a certified leadership and talent management coach) and will provide you with fresh viewpoints, encouraging your growth and development to reach new heights.

Consultant

I have spent more than thirty years in human resources, consulting with rocket scientists, engineers, and many top executives. As a self-described "Translator of the NASA

Way," I know from personal experience that NASA lessons can be applied to a variety of other contexts.

Let me help you build your organizational culture the NASA way—starting with strong core values and expected behaviors and aligning your talent management, rewards, and recognition strategies with your desired culture.

Together, we can design strategies to develop your leaders and improve both your culture and employee engagement. Let's talk about how we can partner on a plan that enables you and your organization to shoot for the stars!

Please contact me on:

LinkedIn: https://www.linkedin.com/in/bradyapyle/

X (Twitter): @BradyPyle

Check out my Blog at https://bradypyle.com/

Bibliography

Buckingham, Marcus, Curt Coffman, Rodd Wagner, and James K. Harter. *12: The Elements of Great Managing*. Washington, DC: Gallup Press, 2006.

Cain, Susan. *Quiet: The Power of Introverts in a World That Can't Stop Talking*. New York, NY: Crown, 2012.

Carrig, Ken, and Patrick Wright. *Building Profit through Building People: Making Your Workforce the Strongest Link in the Value-Profit Chain*. Alexandria, VA: Society for Human Resource Management, 2006.

Chapman, Gary, and Paul White. *The 5 Languages of Appreciation in the Workplace*. Chicago, IL: Northfield Publishing, 2019.

Collins, Alan. *Start Your Own Awesome HR Blog*. Published by the author, 2023.

Covey, Stephen R. *The 7 Habits of Highly Effective People*. New York, NY: Simon & Schuster, 2020.

Covey, Stephen M.R. *Speed of Trust*. New York, NY: Free Press, 2006.

Daly, Peter H., and Michael Watkins. *The First 90 Days in Government: Critical Success Strategies for New Public Managers at All Levels*. Brighton, MA: Harvard Business Review Press, 2006.

Dethloff, Henry C. *Suddenly, Tomorrow Came: The NASA History of the Johnson Space Center.* Garden City, NY: Dover Publications, 2013.

Fine, Alan, and Merrill, Rebecca R. *You Already Know How to Be Great: A Simple Way to Remove Interference and Unlock Your Greatest Potential.* New York, NY: Porfolio, 2010.

Kahnweiler, Jennifer B. *Quiet Influence: The Introvert's Guide to Making a Difference.* Oakland, CA: Berrett-Koehler Publishers, 2013.

Kaye, Beverly. *Love 'Em or Lose 'Em, Getting Good People to Stay.* Oakland, CA: Berrett-Koehler Publishers, 2021.

Kranz, Gene. *Failure Is Not an Option: Mission Control from Mercury to Apollo 13.* New York, NY: Simon & Schuster, 2001.

Maxwell, John. *Good Leaders Ask Great Questions.* Suwanee, GA: The John Maxwell Company, 2014.

Peters, Thomas J., and Robert H. Waterman Jr. *In Search of Excellence: Lessons from America's Best-Run Companies.* Doylestown, PA: Harper Business, 2004.

Ross, Craig, Angela V. Paccione, and Victoria L. Roberts. *Do Big Things: The Simple Steps Teams Can Take to Mobilize Hearts and Minds, and Make an Epic Impact.* Hoboken, NJ: Wiley, 2017.

Schein, Edgar H., and Schein, Peter A. *Humble Inquiry: The Gentle Art of Asking Instead of Telling.* Oakland, CA: Berrett-Koehler Publishers, 2025.

Sinek, Simon. *Leaders Eat Last.* New York, NY: Porfolio, 2014.

Ulrich, David. *Human Resource Champions.* Brighton, MA: Harvard Business Review Press, 1996.

Watkins, Michael. *The First 90 Days: Critical Success Strategies for New Leaders at All Levels.* Brighton, MA: Harvard Business School Press, 2003.

Wright, Patrick M. *The Chief HR Officer: Defining the New Role of Human Resource Leaders.* San Francisco, CA: Jossey-Bass, 2011.

www.ingramcontent.com/pod-product-compliance
Lightning Source LLC
Chambersburg PA
CBHW031622210526
45464CB00004B/1709